Getting Started

With

Windows 95

Getting Started With Windows 95

Sylvia Russakoff
Lynn Marie Bacon
Pace Computer Learning Center
School of Computer Science and Information Systems
Pace University

Babette Kronstadt
David Sachs
Series Editors
Pace Computer Learning Center
School of Computer Science and Information Systems
Pace University

JOHN WILEY & SONS, INC.

New York / Chichester / Brisbane / Toronto / Singapore

Trademark Acknowledgments:

Microsoft is a registered trademark of Microsoft Corporation
Excel for Windows is a trademark of Microsoft Corporation
Word for Windows is a trademark of Microsoft Corporation
PowerPoint for Windows is a trademark of Microsoft Corporation
Microsoft Office is a trademark of Microsoft Corporation
Windows is a trademark of Microsoft Corporation
Windows 95 is a trademark of Microsoft Corporation
Microsoft Access is a registered trademark of Microsoft Corporation
1-2-3 is a registered trademark of Lotus Development Corporation
WordPerfect is a registered trademark of WordPerfect Corporation
IBM is a registered trademark of International Business Machines Corporation
Paradox is a registered trademark of Borland International, Inc.

Portions of this text were adapted from other texts in this series and from Pace University Computer Learning Center manuals.

ISBN 0-471-15943-3

Printed in the United States of America

10 9 8 7 6 5

Printed and bound by Malloy Lithographing, Inc.

Preface

Key Elements

Each lesson in *Getting Started with Windows 95* uses five key elements to help students master specific concepts and skills and develop the ability to apply them.

- **Learning objectives**, located at the beginning of each lesson, focus students on the skills to be learned.

- **Bulleted lists of step-by-step procedures** introduce the tasks and provide a quick reference.

- **Activities with step-by-step instructions** guide students as they apply the general procedures to solve the problems presented by the projects.

- **Screen illustrations** provide visual aids for learning and illustrate major steps.

- **Independent projects** provide opportunities to practice newly acquired skills with decreasing level of support.

Flexible Use

Getting Started with Windows 95 is designed for use in an introductory computer course. As a "getting started" book, it does not attempt to cover all of the possible topics in using *Windows 95*. Rather, it introduces and reinforces the topics that students will be likely to find valuable. While designed to be used in conjunction with lectures or other instructor supervision, concepts are explained clearly enough so that students can use the book in independent learning settings. Students should be able to follow specific instructions with minimal instructor assistance.

Acknowledgments

Getting Started with Windows 95 was written by two of us, but it represents the work and effort of many individuals and organizations. Jessica Kronstadt, Matthew Poli, and Joseph Knowlton performed their usual miracles with the layout, annotation, and text formatting. Babette Kronstadt and Elizabeth Massa read the manuscript and shared their expertise, giving us many valuable suggestions. Nicole Ciafone and Kevin Downey tested and refined the exercises.

We received enormous institutional support from Pace University and the School of Computer Science and Information Systems (CSIS) and its Dean, Dr. Susan Merritt.

From another perspective, this book is also a product of the Pace Computer Learning Center, a loose affiliation of approximately 15 faculty and staff who have provided more than 7,000 days of instruction to over 60,000 individuals in corporate settings throughout the United States and around the world during the past nine years. Our shared experiences in the development and teaching of these non-credit workshops, as well as credit bearing courses through the Pace University School of Computer Science and Information Systems, was an ideal preparation for writing this book. In addition none of our books for John Wiley would have been possible without the continuing support of David Sachs, the director of the Computer Learning Center.

We have received many invaluable comments and suggestions from Jorge Gaytan at the University of Texas, El Paso, who was kind enough to review an early draft of this book.

Our thanks also go to the many people at John Wiley who provided us with support and assistance. Our editor, Beth Lang Golub, associate editor Ellen Ford, and assistant editors Andrea Bryant and David Kear have all been very responsive to our concerns and helpful in all of the Pace Computer Learning Center's writing projects.

Last but not least, we would like to thank our families and friends without whose support and patience we could not have written this book.

Sylvia Russakoff
Lynn Marie Bacon

March, 1996
White Plains, New York

Contents

7   Using the Windows Explorer   135

8   Customizing Windows 95 with Shortcuts 157

Appendix 169

Index   173

Students and Instructors
Before Getting Started Please Note:

A BRIEF OVERVIEW

Getting Started with Windows 95 provides a step-by-step, hands-on introduction to the newest version of Microsoft Windows. It is designed for students who have a working knowledge of the PC, but may or may not have previous experience with *Windows*. Each lesson presents carefully structured material, organized in short, focused activities which build to help the student absorb both conceptual and practical knowledge. Independent projects at the end of each lesson allow students to reinforce and expand their knowledge. Students will gain the most benefit from *Getting Started with Windows 95* if they complete all Activities and Independent Projects.

STUDENT DATA DISKS

Students begin with a blank disk and create their own files in the course of using the book. They are expected to complete all activities and projects in each lesson. Typing has been kept to a minimum. Both activities and projects contain documents that may be printed and submitted to instructors.

ASSIGNMENTS

While learning an operating system, there are many times when a student will manipulate the screen image without creating a file. In *Getting Started with Windows 95,* students are also instructed to print current screen images using the **PRINTSCREEN** key and the Clipboard so that instructors can check their work.

STOP AND GO

The steps for completing each feature introduced in this book are covered twice. First they are described in a bulleted list, which can be used for reference. Then the same steps are used in a hands-on Activity. **Be sure to wait until the Activity to practice each feature on the computer.**

SETUP OF WINDOWS 95

One of the strengths of *Windows 95* is the ease with which the screens and even some of the program's responses to commands can be customized. This, however, can cause problems for students trying to learn how to use the program. This book assumes that *Windows 95* has been installed using the default settings, and that they have not been changed. Some hints are given about where to look if the computer responds differently from the way it would under standard settings. If your screen looks different from one or more in the book, ask your instructor or laboratory assistant to check that the defaults have not been changed.

Introducing Windows 95

Objectives

In this lesson you will learn to:

- Understand what *Windows 95* is
- Recognize the differences between *Windows 95* and *Windows 3.1*
- Run *Windows 95*
- Identify the Desktop icons

- Open and close windows
- Use the mouse
- Move and resize windows
- Use menus and dialog boxes
- Shut down *Windows 95*

BEGINNING WINDOWS VOCABULARY

Window	A four-sided frame within which a program, document or message to the user is enclosed. Almost everything you do in the *Windows* environment will take place inside a window.
Icon	A small picture used to represent a program or document.
Desktop	The background screen of *Windows 95* which holds all icons and windows.
Mouse	A small hand-held device used for giving commands to the computer.
Operating system	A type of software program that every computer must have. It works behind the scenes to direct the flow of data in the computer, and makes it possible for you to organize and manage your documents.

Table 1 - 1

WHAT IS WINDOWS 95?

Windows 95 is the newest version of *Windows*, the program from Microsoft Corporation that lets you organize, run, and manage your programs and documents at the computer. Over the last few years, *Windows* has grown tremendously in importance and is now the standard operating system for IBM and other compatible brands of personal computers.

What features characterize the *Windows* environment? Some of the most important are:

Graphical User Interface	*Windows 95* uses images called *icons* to represent the programs, documents, commands, and other parts of the computer system. The user employs the *mouse* as a device for giving commands to the computer.
"Look" and "Feel"	All windows contain many of the same elements. Basic tasks like saving and printing are done in the same way in all programs.
Sharing of Set-up Information	*Windows* sets up your printer, keyboard, monitor, fax, and any other devices you use, and shares this information with all your programs.
Multi-tasking	You may work with as many programs at one time as the capacity of your computer will allow.
Transfer and integration of information	You can assemble a document that contains parts that have been created in many different programs by copying, moving, embedding and linking data.

Table 1 - 2

WHAT'S NEW ABOUT WINDOWS 95?

If you are switching to *Windows 95* from a previous version of *Windows*, you are probably wondering about the changes you will encounter. The most important change is one that is invisible. *Windows 95* is a full-fledged operating system, and handles all operating system functions, while earlier versions of *Windows* required the presence of the DOS operating system installed separately on the computer. *Windows 95* is faster than earlier versions of *Windows*, and works behind the scenes with fewer crashes and delays. During installation, the new **Plug and Play** feature recognizes your hardware and sets it up automatically.

The visible changes in *Windows 95* include both new features and improvements to old features, all of which make *Windows* easier to use. When you turn on your computer you will see a simple, clean Desktop containing only a few icons. You may customize the Desktop to include additional icons if you wish. You will find it easier to open, close, maximize, and minimize windows. Programs are easier to find and run from the new Start menu and Taskbar, and can be saved with long filenames. You can manage documents and disks with the new Windows Explorer, which replaces the File Manager. Documents may be deleted and undeleted easily by using the Recycle Bin. You can enjoy using the improved communications features that support e-mail, faxing, and the Internet. If you are using *Windows 95* on a network you can make use of its new network features.

WHAT IF I'VE NEVER USED WINDOWS?

This book assumes that although you have a basic familiarity with the personal computer, you are a new *Windows* user. It will introduce the vocabulary and concepts you need to master, familiarize you with the use of the mouse, and guide you in your exploration of the *Windows* environment. You will need a new, formatted 3.5" floppy disk that we will call the *data disk* to use with this book.[*] When you use the disk, label it carefully and don't lose it, as you will need it for almost every lesson. In addition to the activities you will complete as you work through this book, you will find Independent Projects to reinforce and extend your skills at the conclusion of each lesson.

RUNNING WINDOWS 95

Every computer must have an operating system, and *Windows 95* is now the operating system for your computer. To run *Windows 95*, all you need to do is turn on your computer!

---

[*] If you cannot obtain a formatted disk, see Appendix 1.

Instructions for all activities:

- Read and follow each numbered instruction.
- Read italicized text also. It provides additional information you will need.
- Read **PROBLEM SOLVERS** only if you cannot proceed.

Activity 1.1: Running Windows 95

1. Turn on your personal computer.

   The boot-up procedure may take longer than you expect. Make sure there is no disk in the floppy drive or you will get an error message.

   Some systems display a Welcome screen before the Desktop appears.

   If you are using Windows 95 on a network, you may be asked to sign on. You will have to type your User ID and password. If you need help, ask your instructor or lab assistant.

2. You will see the Desktop, the opening screen of *Windows 95*. Your monitor screen should look similar to Figure 1-1. Your screen may not match the figure exactly because the setup of *Windows 95* may vary from one computer to another.

Figure 1 - 1   The Windows 95 Desktop

PROBLEM SOLVER:: *If the Windows 95 Desktop does not appear, your computer may have been set to run a different program or a different operating system when you boot up. Ask you instructor or lab assistant for help.*

3. Leave the computer on for the next activity.

USING THE MOUSE

You need to learn to use the mouse before you begin to explore *Windows 95*. If you can use the mouse comfortably, you may skip to the next section, *What is on the Desktop?*

You may notice that the mouse pointer takes different shape onscreen depending upon what you are doing. It may appear as a single or double-headed arrow, a slender vertical line, a pointing finger or a small cross. While most people enjoy using the mouse once they have mastered it, keyboard alternatives exist for all commands. You may wish to try some of them (see Appendix 2).

Most *Windows 95* features are covered in two ways. First, they are described in a **bulleted** list. **Read** the bulleted instructions carefully. Then, the features are practiced in a hands-on *Activity*. **Carry out** the **numbered** instructions in the *Activity* on your computer. Remember **not** to carry out the bulleted items on your computer. The icon in the margin will remind you to wait for the *Activities* before carrying out instructions on your computer.

To hold and move the mouse:

- Put the palm of your hand on the mouse.

- Slide the mouse around the mouse pad or flat surface next to your computer. The mouse must be guided by the palm of your hand, *not* by your fingers.

To Use the Mouse:

Point	Touch the point of the arrow to a spot on the screen
	Pointing is used to position your mouse pointer for the next action. It is important to touch the object you are pointing to. It is best to get near the center of the object rather than the edge.
Click	Lightly press and immediately release the *left* mouse button. Occasionally, the right mouse button will be specified. At all other times, use the left button.
	Clicking is used to highlight or select an object so that the following action taken will affect it. Clicking also opens and closes menus, and can close or resize a window.
Drag	Point to an object on-screen, press the mouse button and hold it down, and then slide the mouse. The object you are pointing to will move on-screen along with the mouse arrow.
	Dragging is used to highlight text in documents and to move and copy text.
Double-click	Click and release the mouse button twice in rapid succession. Click quickly and lightly. Do not move the mouse as you click.
	Double-clicking is used to open windows and run programs.

Table 1 - 3

WHAT IS ON THE DESKTOP?

The icons on the *Windows 95* Desktop may vary slightly, depending on how your computer was set up (see Table 1-4). These brief descriptions will be expanded as you read Lessons 1 and 2.

Activity 1.2: Using the Mouse
In this activity you will practice using the mouse. Don't worry about not understanding the tasks you are completing. They will be explained later in this lesson, or in Lesson 2.

1. Turn on your computer, if it is not already on.

   You should see the Windows 95 Desktop pictured in Figure 1-1.

2. Place the palm of your right hand on the mouse and move it slowly on the mouse pad or flat surface. Watch the movement of the mouse pointer onscreen.

The index finger of your right hand should rest easily on the left mouse button.

If you are left-handed, switch the mouse to the left side of the computer and try to hold it with your left hand. If this is difficult, don't worry. You will learn to use the left-handed mouse setting in Lesson 3.

	My Computer	My Computer contains the contents of the drives on your computer.
	Inbox	The Inbox holds the electronic mail messages you have sent and received using Microsoft Exchange.
	Network Neighborhood	This icon appears if your computer is connected to a network. It contains all the computers that are part of the network.
	Recycle Bin	The Recycle Bin is used to hold files you are planning to delete. The files are held in the Recycle Bin until you either delete them or restore them.
	Microsoft Network	Microsoft Network is a new online service offered to all *Windows 95* users. It provides connectivity to the Internet and many other features.
	My Briefcase	The Briefcase helps you keep important files up to date when you work on them on the road and at your home or office. It is installed if you choose the Portable option or the Custom option during the Windows 95 setup.
	Start	The Start icon, or button, is your gateway to the programs, documents, settings, and all other features on your computer. It is located on the Taskbar.
	Taskbar	The Taskbar extends from the Start button across the bottom of the screen to the clock. It displays the name of all open windows in *Windows 95*.

Table 1 - 4

3. Point to the icon labeled **My Computer**.

   Remember to touch the arrow point to the icon (see Figure 1-2).

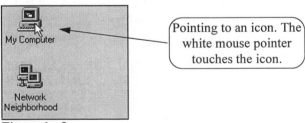

Pointing to an icon. The white mouse pointer touches the icon.

Figure 1 - 2

4. Point to the **Start** button at the lower left corner of your screen.

   PROBLEM SOLVER: *If the Start button is not visible, point to the bottom of the screen, and the button will appear.*

5. Point to the **Recycle Bin**.

6. Keeping your mouse pointer on the **Recycle Bin**, click the left mouse button. Keep your hand steady as you click.

Both the icon and its label will change color. The icon is now selected. You will learn more about selected objects later.

PROBLEM SOLVER: *If the mouse does not work, or works incorrectly, its settings may have been changed. Ask your instructor for assistance.*

7. Click on a blank part of the Desktop to unselect the Recycle Bin icon.

8. Click on the **My Computer** icon to select it.

9. Click on a blank part of the Desktop to unselect the icon.

10. Point to the **Start** button in the lower left corner of your screen. When you see the single-headed arrow on the Start button, click the mouse.

    The Start menu will open (see Figure 1-3).

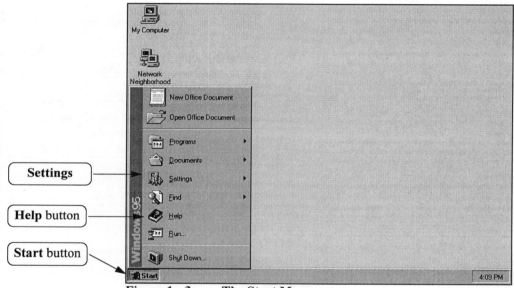

Figure 1 - 3   The Start Menu

11. Point to the item on the menu marked **Help** and click. Notice that **Help** is highlighted automatically when you point to it. This represents a change from earlier versions of *Windows*.

    You have opened the Windows 95 Help feature. You will learn to use Help in Lesson 4.

12. To close **Help**, click on the button marked **Cancel** in the lower right corner of the Help window (see Figure 1-4).

13. Click on the **Start** button again.

14. Now point to the **Settings** button (see Figure 1-3). Notice the triangle pointing to the right.

    The triangle indicates that Settings contains another list of choices. As you point to Settings, a smaller list containing three items opens to its right.

15. Point to one of the choices, **Control Panel**, and click. Before you click, your screen should resemble Figure 1-5.

    A new window, the Windows 95 Control Panel, will open. The Control Panel contains a group of programs, each represented by an icon. These programs control many of the settings that are part of Windows 95.

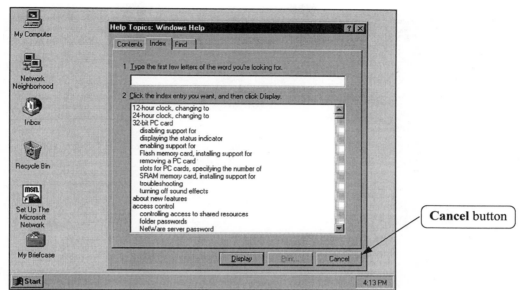

Figure 1 - 4   **Clicking on the Cancel Button**

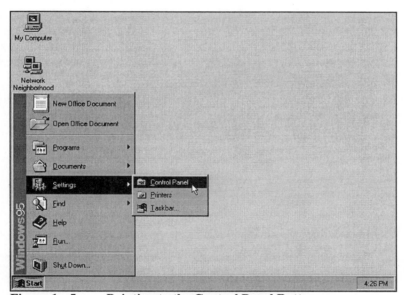

Figure 1 - 5   **Pointing to the Control Panel Button**

16. To make sure the Control Panel window is large enough for you to see all its icons, click on the Maximize button, to the left of the **X** in the upper right corner of the window. You will learn more about this button later in the lesson.

17. To open the program in the Control Panel that controls the date and time, double-click on the **Date/Time** icon. Remember to click twice - quickly and lightly, without moving your hand.

    If you see an icon representing an hourglass, this means that Windows 95 is working on your command. Be patient.

    The Date/Time window will open (see Figure 1-6).

18. To close the **Date/Time** window, point to the **X** (the Close button) in the upper right corner of its window and click (see Figure 1-6).

Figure 1 - 6   Clicking the Correct Close Button

PROBLEM SOLVER: *If the Control Panel window closes and the Date/Time window does not, you clicked the X in the wrong window (See Figure 1 - 6   Clicking the Correct Close Button). Be sure to click the X in the corner of the correct window. Leave the Control Panel window closed for now and skip Step 19.*

19. To close the Control Panel window, click the **Close** button in the upper right corner of the Control Panel window.

    You will learn about the Control Panel in Lesson 3.

20. Close any other window that may be open by clicking on its **Close** button.

21. Leave your computer on for the next activity.

PARTS OF A WINDOW

Figure 1-7 shows the elements of a typical *Windows 95* window. You will become familiar with each part in the remainder of this lesson and in Lesson 2. Refer back to this figure whenever you need to identify part of a window.

OPENING, CLOSING, MOVING AND SIZING WINDOWS

During the last activity, you had two windows open on your Desktop—the Control Panel window and the Date/Time window. As you work in *Windows 95*, your Desktop will often be filled with many open windows—a state that confuses newcomers to the *Windows* scene! To feel comfortable in *Windows 95*, you will need to be able to be able to open and close windows easily, as well as move them around the Desktop and change their size.

To open a window:

• Point to an icon on the Desktop or in a window.

• Double-click.

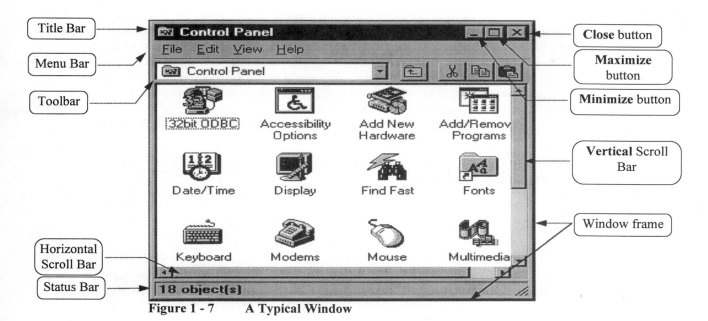

Title Bar

Menu Bar

Toolbar

Horizontal Scroll Bar

Status Bar

Close button

Maximize button

Minimize button

Vertical Scroll Bar

Window frame

Figure 1 - 7   A Typical Window

To close a window:

- Point to the **Close** button ![X] in the upper right corner of the window.
- Click.

To move a window:

- Drag the **Title bar** of the window to the new location (see Figure 1-7 for location of the Title bar).

    The Title bar is the colored band at the top of a window that contains its name.

To size a window:

- Point to one of the four sides of the window frame, or to one of the four corners of the window.

    When the mouse touches the window frame it changes to a double-headed arrow. Do not proceed until you see the double-headed arrow.

- Drag the window frame (see Figure 1-7) to resize the window.

    Dragging one of the four sides will move only that side, while dragging one of the corners will move two sides of the window at once.

MAXIMIZING, MINIMIZING, AND RESTORING WINDOWS

By sizing a window you can set its dimensions exactly, and by moving a window you can position it precisely. However, there are two pre-set sizes for windows— **Maximized** and **Minimized**— that can be chosen by clicking one of the two buttons directly to the left of the **X** that closes the window. See Figure 1-7 for the location of these buttons.

A *maximized* window fills the entire screen. You saw this in Step 16 of the last Activity. This setting gives you the best view of the window's contents, but a maximized window blocks all other windows.

When a window is *minimized*, its name still appears on the Taskbar but its contents cannot be seen. The window can be restored to its previous size by a single mouse click. The size of a *restored* window is between maximized and minimized size.

When a window is *restored*, it returns from maximized, minimized, or closed to its previous size.

To maximize a window:

- Click on the Maximize button ▣ which is the middle button at the right end of the Title Bar.

To restore a window:

- If a window has already been maximized, it will not contain a Maximize button, but will contain a Restore button 🗗 instead. Clicking on the Restore button will return a window to its previous size.

To minimize a window:

- Click on the Minimize button ▬ to the left of the Maximize/Restore button.

Activity 1.3: Working with Windows on the Desktop

In this activity, you will open, close, size, and move windows. Do not be concerned if you are asked to look at parts of *Windows 95* that are new to you. They will be explained shortly.

1. Turn on your computer, if it is not already on.

2. At the Desktop, point to the icon called **My Computer**.

3. Double-click on the icon. Figure 1 - 8 shows the **My Computer** window with *large icons* displayed. If your screen does not match the figure, at the Menu Bar click on **View** and then click on **Large Icons**.

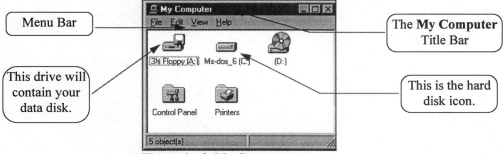

Figure 1 - 8 My Computer

PROBLEM SOLVER: *If the window does not open, double-click again, being careful not to move the mouse as you click. If the window still does not open, click on the icon once and press ENTER.*

If the window fills the entire screen, click the **Restore** *button near the upper right corner of the window to make it smaller.*

4. Click and drag the Title bar of the window (Figure 1-8) to move it to a different place onscreen.

   When you start to drag, the outline of the window will appear. Position the outline where you want the window moved and release the mouse button.

5. Touch any one of the four sides of the window with the mouse pointer.

   You should see the mouse change to a double-headed arrow.

6. Change the size of the window by dragging one of its four sides.

7. Touch one of the four *corners* of the window with the mouse pointer and drag to change the window's size.

   When the double-headed arrow is positioned diagonally, you will be changing both dimensions (height and width) simultaneously.

8. Within the **My Computer** window, point to the icon of the hard disk of your computer (**C:**) and double-click.

   A second window will open that lists the folders (directories) and files saved on the C: drive. This window may be bigger or smaller than the **My Computer** *window.*

 PROBLEM SOLVER*: If this new window covers the entire screen, follow the instructions in italics at the end of Step 3.*

 PROBLEM SOLVER*: If there is no picture of the hard drive, this may have been deliberately hidden when Windows 95 was set up in your lab. Double-click on another icon instead and continue with Step 9.*

9. Size and move the two windows next to each other so that they do not overlap (see Figure 1-9).

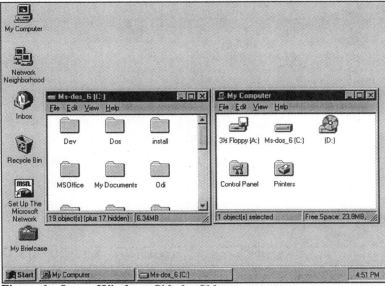

Figure 1 - 9   **Windows Side by Side**

It will take at least several maneuvers to accomplish this. Take your time. Resize the windows so they are the same size, following the instructions above, and then move one window at a time until they are next to each other.

PROBLEM SOLVER: *If one window covers the other, move the one in front aside by dragging its Title Bar.*

10. Click the **X** in the upper right corner of the **My Computer** window to close it.

11. Click the **X** in the upper right corner of the hard disk (**C:**) window to close it.

    The Desktop should have no windows open at this point.

12. Leave the computer running for the next activity.

Activity 1.4: Using Maximize, Minimize and Restore

1. Turn on your computer, if it is not already on.

2. At the Desktop, double-click on the **Recycle Bin** icon (see Figure 1-10).

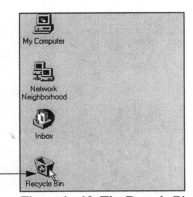

Recycle Bin icon

Figure 1 - 10 The Recycle Bin Icon

The Recycle Bin window opens.

3. Click the Maximize button on the Recycle Bin window, if it is showing. If not, continue with Step 4.

4. Click the Restore button. Remember that both buttons occupy the same location.

   Now the Recycle Bin window returns to its original size.

5. Click the Minimize button.

   *The **Recycle Bin** window is minimized. All that is visible is its name on the Taskbar, at the bottom of the screen. This lets you know that the Recycle Bin has not been closed.*

6. Click on the words: **Recycle Bin** on the Taskbar to restore the window to its previous size.

7. Leave the Recycle Bin and double-click on the **My Computer** icon to open it.

PROBLEM SOLVER: *If the **My Computer** icon is not visible, it may be hidden by the **Recycle Bin** window. Move the Recycle Bin window aside.*

8. In the **My Computer** window, double-click on the icon for the Control Panel.

   This is the same window that you opened from the Start menu in the last activity.

PROBLEM SOLVER: *If the **Control Panel** icon is not visible, increase the size of the **My Computer** window.*

9. Maximize the Control Panel window if it is not already maximized. Notice how other windows are covered by the maximized window.

   Notice that all open windows are listed on the Taskbar.

10. Close the Control Panel window.

    The other windows are uncovered.

11. Close the **My Computer** window.

12. Close the **Recycle Bin** window and any other windows that are open.

    PROBLEM SOLVER: *If the Close button is not visible on any of these windows, drag the window by the title bar until you can see the X.*

13. Leave the computer running for the next activity.

MENUS AND DIALOG BOXES

In addition to working with icons, buttons and windows, you will be using menus and dialog boxes to give commands to your computer.

A *menu* is a list of commands (see Figure 1-7). When you click on a menu, a list of commands drops down onto your screen (hence the term *drop-down menu*). You then click on the command of your choice. Not every window has a menu. When a window contains a menu you will find it directly below the Title Bar. Some menu commands have keyboard shortcuts associated with them, and these shortcuts are noted on the menus.

Usually, clicking on a menu command will cause the computer to carry out that command immediately, but sometimes it needs more data first. A *dialog box* is a small window that opens automatically, containing areas where you can provide more information to the computer. The dialog box may contain areas in which to type, lists to select from, boxes to check, and buttons to push.

To use a menu:

- Point to the menu name (e.g. **File)** on the Menu Bar and click to open (see Figure 1-11).

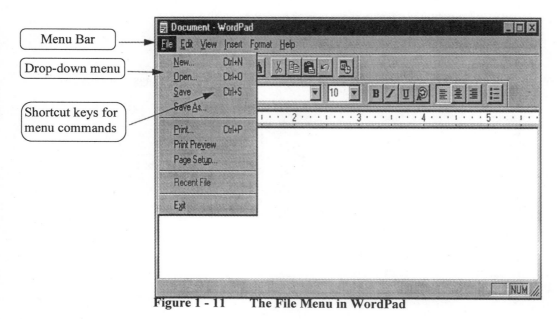

Figure 1 - 11   The File Menu in WordPad

- To choose a command from the menu, point to the word on the menu and click.

ALTERNATE MOUSE METHOD: *Keep the mouse button down when you click on the menu name and drag down the menu, releasing the button at the command you want.*

- To close a menu, click again on the menu name on the Menu Bar.

Using Menus with the Keyboard

Although you may be comfortable with the mouse by now, you should also learn the keystrokes for using a menu. In situations where your hands are on the keyboard, you may appreciate being able to control the menus directly from the keyboard without having to reach for the mouse.

To use a menu with the keyboard:

- To activate the Menu Bar, press the **ALT** key (found on either side of the **SPACEBAR**).
- Tap the underlined letter of the menu of your choice (e.g. the **F** on the File menu).

  The menu will open, meaning that a list of commands will drop down onto your screen.

- To choose a command, tap the underlined letter of the command or use the keyboard shortcut listed on the menu.
- To close a menu, press the **ESC** key (in the upper left corner of the keyboard). This closes the menu that is open, but keeps the Menu Bar activated in case you want to use a different menu.
- To de-activate the Menu Bar, press the **ALT** key again.

As you look at a drop-down menu, you will see that certain commands appear in gray, not black characters. The gray characters mean that a command is currently unavailable. Some commands are followed by a series of three dots called an *ellipsis*. Such commands cannot be carried out until more information is given to the computer. When you choose a command followed by an ellipsis, a dialog box will open so that you can enter the information the computer needs. Dialog boxes may be controlled with either the mouse or keyboard. Keyboard shortcuts for controlling dialog boxes may be found in Appendix 2.

To use a dialog box:

- When a dialog box opens, use the following procedures to change the settings to meet your needs (see Figure 1-12).

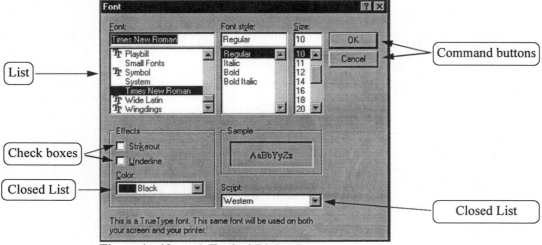

Figure 1 - 12   A Typical Dialog Box

o   You can type in the **text box** areas (not displayed);

o   Select items from **closed** and **open lists** by clicking on the item of your choice. If only one item is visible, click on the ↓ to open the list. If less than the entire list is visible, you may click the ↓ and ↑ next to the list to move up and down. This is called *scrolling* the list;

o   If there is a set of **check boxes** (square), click on the appropriate one(s). You may select as many as you wish, or none at all. If a box is checked, you may click on it again to uncheck it;

o   If there is a set of **radio buttons** (round), click on the appropriate one. Because only one may be selected at a time, clicking on one removes the previous selection (not displayed);

o   Some dialog boxes have more than one panel. Click on the appropriate **index tab** to reach the screen of your choice;

•   You may use the mouse or the **TAB** key to move from one section of the box to another.

•   When the dialog box has been filled in correctly, click **OK** to carry out the instructions, or **Cancel** to remove the dialog box. The **OK** and **Cancel** buttons are called **command buttons**.

KEYBOARD ALTERNATIVE: *Instead of clicking on* **OK**, *you may press* **ENTER**. *Instead of clicking on* **Cancel**, *you may press the* **ESC** *key, in the upper left corner of your keyboard.*

•   If you need help with the dialog box, click on the **Help** button. A Help window will open which describes each element of the dialog box and gives instructions for completing it.

Activity 1.5: Using Menus and Dialog Boxes

In this activity you will open the **My Computer** window and work with its **View** and **Help** menus and dialog boxes. If any terms are unfamiliar to you, refer back to Figure 1-7.

1.   Turn on your computer, if it is not already on.

2.   At the Desktop, double-click on the **My Computer** icon. Is the Toolbar showing?

The Toolbar, a row of buttons positioned below the Menu Bar may or may not appear.

3.   Maximize the window, if necessary, by clicking on its Maximize button.

4.   At the Menu Bar, click on the word **View** to open the **View** menu. Is there a check next to **Toolbar**?

If so, the Toolbar is displayed. If not, the Toolbar is not displayed. The display of the Toolbar is turned on and off by clicking on the Toolbar command on the View menu.

5.   If there is no check, click on **Toolbar**. If there is a check, click on **View** to close the menu.

The Toolbar will be displayed.

6.   Click on the **View** menu again and see if there is a check in front of the **Status Bar** command.

7.   If there is no check, click on **Status Bar**. If there is a check, click on **View** to close the menu.

The Status Bar will be displayed at the bottom of the window, directly above the Taskbar. It displays additional information about the contents of the window.

8.   Click on **View** again and examine the next four menu items, which refer to the window's contents: **Large icons**, **Small icons**, **List**, and **Details**.

9.   Click on **View** and make sure **Large Icons** has been selected.

Notice the appearance of the window with large icons displayed.

10. Click on **View** and click on **Small Icons**.

    Notice the difference between large and small icons.

11. Click on **View** and click on **List**.

    List arranges the icons in a vertical list.

12. Click on **View** and click on **Details**.

    Details adds information about the icons.

13. Now that you have examined all the choices, return to **Large Icons**.

14. At the Menu Bar, click on **HELP**.

15. Click on **About Windows 95**.

16. Read the screen and click on **OK**.

17. At the Menu Bar, click on **VIEW/Options**.

    The format VIEW/Options (or MENU/Command) will be used frequently. It means that you should click on the View menu and then click on the Options command.

18. Click on the index tab marked **Folder**.

    This opens the Folder panel of the dialog box.

19. Under the heading **Browsing Options**, click each of the two buttons. Only one button at a time may be selected.

20. Leave the top button selected.

21. At the top of the dialog box, click on the **View** index tab.

22. Under the heading **Hide files of these types:** click on the ↓ to scroll the list of files.

23. Click the square check box next to the words **Display the full MS-DOS path in the title bar** at least twice to see the check mark appear and disappear.

24. Leave the box unchecked.

25. Click on the third index tab, **File Types**.

26. Scroll the list of registered file types. Notice the different icon for each type of file.

27. Click on different file types on the list and notice how the **File type details** below the list change.

28. Click on the **Cancel** button at the bottom of the dialog box to close the box without saving any of the changes you made.

29. Close the **My Computer** window.

CLOSING WINDOWS 95

Don't shut your computer down merely by turning it off! When you exit improperly from *Windows 95*, certain files that are supposed to be deleted when you exit the program are not, and instead stay permanently on your system. Sooner or later this will cause problems. To exit from *Windows 95*, you will need to use the Start button at the bottom of the screen.

To exit from Windows 95:

- Click on the Start button **Start** at the bottom of the screen.

If the button is not visible, point to the bottom left corner of the screen.

- Click on the **Shut Down** command.

- When the **Shut Down Windows** dialog box appears, click on the **Yes** button.

- Turn off your computer when you see the message that says you may do so.

Activity 1.6: Closing Windows 95

1. Close any windows that are open.

2. Click on the **Start** button.

3. Click on **Shut Down** and **Yes** in the Shut Down Windows dialog box (see Figure 1 - 13).

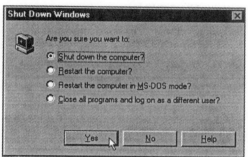

Figure 1 - 13 Shutting Down the Computer

4. Turn off your computer when you are permitted to do so.

SUMMARY

Lesson 1 has given you a basic orientation to *Windows 95*. You learned the advantages of being a user of *Windows 95*, and the differences between it and the previous version of *Windows*. Then, you practiced the techniques for operating the mouse and became familiar with the icons you see on the Desktop when you first turn on *Windows 95*. After practicing opening and closing windows, you worked with windows that were Maximized, Minimized and Restored. You then practiced handling menus and dialog boxes. Finally, you learned the proper way to shut down *Windows 95*.

KEY TERMS

C:	Hard drive	Open list
Cancel	Icon	Operating System
Check boxes	Inbox	Plug and Play
Click	List	Point
Closed List	Maximize	Radio buttons
Command buttons	Menu	Recycle Bin
Control Panel	Microsoft Network	Restore
Desktop	Minimize	Start button
Dialog box	Mouse	Taskbar
Double-click	Multi-tasking	Text box
Drag	My Briefcase	Window
Drop-down list	My Computer	
Graphical User Interface	Network Neighborhood	

INDEPENDENT PROJECTS

The independent projects at the conclusion of each lesson will give you additional practice in using the skills you have learned, and will also give you a chance to learn new skills on your own.

Independent Project 1.1: Working with Windows

In this activity, you will reinforce the techniques you learned to open, close, and size windows and work with dialog boxes.

1. Turn on your computer.

2. At the *Windows 95* Desktop, click on the **Start** button.

3. Point to **Settings**, and then click on **Taskbar**.

    *The **Taskbar Properties** dialog box will open (see Figure 1 - 14).*

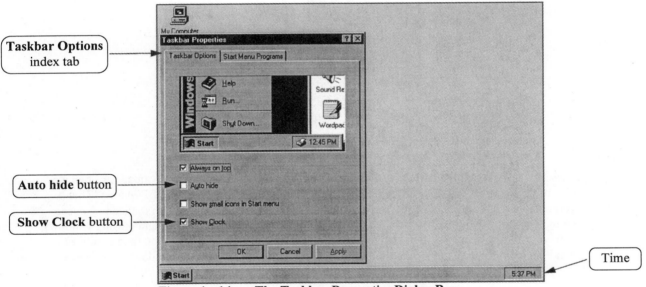

Figure 1 - 14   The Taskbar Properties Dialog Box

4. The **Taskbar Options** index tab should be selected. If not, click on it.

5. Look at the checkbox marked **Show Clock**. Is it checked?

    If the box is checked, you will be able to see the current time on the Taskbar, in the lower right corner of your screen. If the box is not checked, you will not see the time.

6. If the box is empty, leave it alone. If the box has a check, click on the box to remove the check.

7. Click on **OK** at the bottom of the dialog box.

    The Taskbar now does not display the time.

8. To display the time again, repeat steps 2 - 5. Click on the **Show Clock** check box to place a check in it.

9. Click on OK again.

You will see the time displayed.

10. At the Desktop, double-click on the **My Computer** icon.

11. If the window is maximized when it opens, Restore it.

12. In the **My Computer** window, double-click on the **Printers** icon.

*Notice that the new window (**Printers**) is **active**. Its Title Bar is darker than **My Computer's**. It may or may not partially or completely cover the **My Computer** window.*

13. If the **Printers** window is maximized, Restore it.

14. Reduce the size of the **Printers** window further by dragging one or more sides of the window frame. If it blocks **My Computer**, move it aside.

15. To make **My Computer** the active window, click on its name on the Taskbar.

*Notice the change in color of the **My Computer** Title Bar and the **My Computer** button on the Taskbar.*

16. Now click on **Printers** in the Taskbar to make it the active window.

17. Move each window by dragging its Title Bar, so that the windows are as far away from each other as possible.

18. Close the **Printers** window by clicking on its Close button.

19. In the **My Computer** window, double-click on the icon for the hard drive (**C:**).

   PROBLEM SOLVER: *The full name for the hard drive varies from computer to computer.*

   If this icon has been hidden during the Windows 95 setup in your lab, double-click on a different icon and continue with Step 20.

20. Maximize the **C:** window (see Figure 1-15).

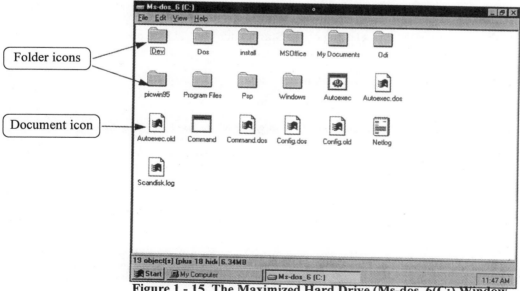

Figure 1 - 15 The Maximized Hard Drive (Ms-dos_6(C:) Window

*The hard drive window has **Large Icons** selected at the **View** menu. It contains icons for folders, which can contain many files, and icons for single documents. You will learn more about these as you work through the book.*

21. Minimize the hard drive window by clicking on its Minimize button.

*Notice the difference between the names on the Taskbar. The active window (**My Computer**) button is brighter in color than the inactive and minimized window (**C:**) (see Figure 1-16).*

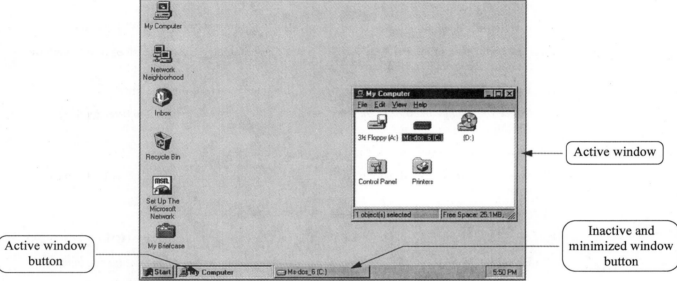

Figure 1 - 16

22. Close the **My Computer** window.

23. Restore the **C:** window by clicking on its name on the Taskbar.

24. Close the **C:** window.

25. Shut down your computer by clicking on the **Start** button and clicking on **Shut Down**.

26. Click on **Yes**.

27. Turn off the computer when you are allowed to do so.

Independent Project 1.2: More Practice with Menus and Dialog boxes

In this activity, you will explore the menus and dialog boxes of two games, Minesweeper and Solitaire, that are included with *Windows 95*.

1. Turn on your computer.

2. At the *Windows 95* Desktop, click on the **Start** button.

3. Point to **Programs**.

4. Moving steadily to the right, point to **Accessories**, then to **Games**, and then click on **Minesweeper**.

   Minesweeper is one of the games included with Windows 95.

5. On the Minesweeper Menu Bar look for the **Game** menu and click on it.

6. Which level game has a check next to it? Beginner? Intermediate?

7. Click on **Intermediate**.

8. Change the level of the game to **Beginner** (see Figure 1-17).

9. Change the level of the game to **Expert**.

10. Click on the **Game** menu, and click on **Custom...**

    The Custom dialog box opens.

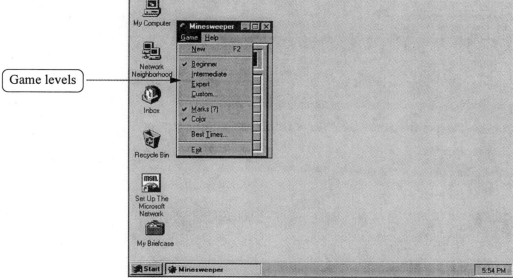

Figure 1 - 17   The Minesweeper Game Menu

11. Position the mouse pointer in the box next to the word **Height**. When the mouse pointer is in the box it will look like a slender I.

12. Click and drag the mouse across the number in the box (see Figure 1-18).

    The number will be selected (shaded).

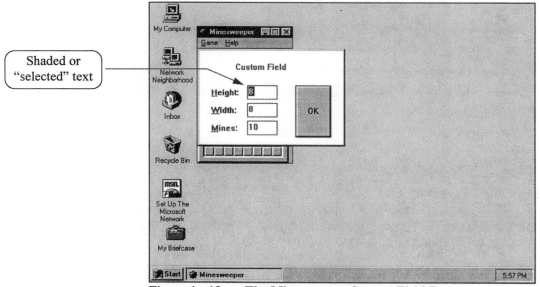

Figure 1 - 18   The Minesweeper Custom Field Box

13. Type the number **20** in the box. It will replace the current number.

14. Change the width to **25** in the same way.

15. Change the number of mines to **30**.

16. Click on **OK**.

17. In the Minesweeper window, notice the number **30** under the Menu Bar. This refers to the number of mines you set.

18. Open the **Game** menu again and click on **Best Times**. Click on OK.

19. To learn the rules for playing Minesweeper, click on the **Help** menu.

20. Click on **Search for Help On...**

21. Make sure the **Index** tab has been selected.

22. Click on **Playing the game** (listed under 2...)

23. Click on **Display**.

24. **Playing the Game** should now be highlighted.

25. Click on **Display**.

    Instructions for playing Minesweeper will be displayed.

26. Maximize the **Minesweeper Help** window and read the instructions for playing.

27. Close the **Help** screen.

    *Now you can play **Minesweeper** whenever you have time.*

28. Close **Minesweeper**.

29. Return to the Start button and this time open the game **Solitaire**.

30. Open the **Game** menu and click on **Deck**.

31. Change to a different card back pattern by clicking on one of the displayed patterns and clicking on **OK**.

32. Click on the **Game** menu and click on **Options**.

33. Explore the **Options** dialog box and then click on **OK**.

34. Open the Help menu and search for Help on playing Solitaire.

35. Read the instructions for playing the game.

36. Close the Help screen(s) and close Solitaire.

    Now you are comfortable with both games. You may play them to relax and have fun with Windows 95.

37. Close any open windows and shut down *Windows 95*.

Independent Project 1.3: Working with multiple windows

In this activity, you will work more independently, exploring Tiled and Cascaded windows. This topic will be covered again in the following lesson. If you cannot remember how to do a particular task, refer to the bulleted instructions in Lesson 1.

1. Turn on your computer.

2. At the Desktop, open the **My Computer** window.

3. At the **My Computer** window, double-click the hard drive (**C:**) icon.

   If this window is not available, proceed without it to Step 5.

4. If the **C:** window is maximized, Restore it.

5. Move the **C:** window aside, if necessary, and at the **My Computer** window, double-click on the **Printers** icon.

6. If the **Printers** window is maximized, Restore it.

7. Move the **Printers** window aside, if necessary, and at the **My Computer** window, double-click on the **Control Panel** icon.

8. If the **Control Panel** window is maximized, Restore it.

   At this point you will have four windows open. The screen is bound to look confusing.

9. Point to the button for each of the open windows on the Taskbar.

   If you can't find the Taskbar, refer to Figure 1-7.

10. Point to an empty area of the Taskbar and click the *right mouse button.*

    An empty area is an area that is not covered by a button. It can be very small. There will always be a small empty area to the left of the clock.

11. With the left mouse button, click on **Tile Horizontally**.

    The windows are arranged so that each occupies a fraction of the screen.

12. Make each window active in turn, by clicking on its Title Bar.

13. Click the *right mouse button* on an empty spot on the Taskbar again, and with the left button, click on **Cascade**.

    When the windows are cascaded, you can see the Title Bar of each, and a full view of the window in front.

14. Click the *right mouse button* on an empty area of the Taskbar again, and click on **Undo Cascade** with the left mouse button.

15. Maximize the Control Panel window.

16. Close the Control Panel window.

17. Close the Printers window.

18. Close all other open windows.

19. Shut down *Windows 95*.

Windows 95 Basics

Objectives

In this lesson you will learn how to:

- Run a program in *Windows 95*
- Run multiple programs
- Understand and use the Start menu
- Cascade and Tile windows
- Understand and use the Taskbar

- Change the Taskbar settings
- Perform basic tasks in the *Windows 95* environment
- Use the *Windows 95* Clipboard

THE START MENU

The Start menu is new to *Windows 95*. It is the gateway to all the programs that have been installed on your computer. Its button usually appears in the lower left corner of the Desktop.

The Start menu makes it easy to run programs. In *Windows 3.1*, before you could run a program you needed to first find its program group. Often, you would open many program groups as you searched for the right one. Now, when you click on the **Start** button and click on **Programs**, a list of your installed programs and program groups will open, and you can locate your program by pointing, without having to open and close additional windows.

The Start menu also provides access to other features, for example the **Help** feature, the **Find** feature, the **Settings** feature, and the **Shut Down** feature, used when you turn off your computer. In a later lesson, we will learn to add shortcuts to the Start menu so that you can reach your programs and documents even more quickly.

Activity 2.1: Opening the Start Menu

In this activity, you will open and examine the **Start** menu.

1. Turn on your computer, if necessary.

2. Click on the *Windows 95* **Start** button and point to **Programs**.

   *When you click on the **Start** button and point to **Programs**, your screen will look similar to Figure 2-1.*

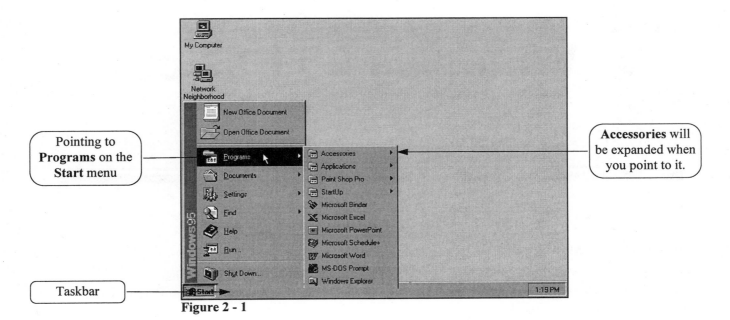

Pointing to **Programs** on the **Start** menu

Accessories will be expanded when you point to it.

Taskbar

Figure 2 - 1

Your list of programs may not look exactly like the one in Figure 2-1 because different programs may have been installed on your computer.

Notice the triangles that point to the right next to some of the listings. They tell you that the listing will be expanded in an adjacent panel (see Figure 2-2).

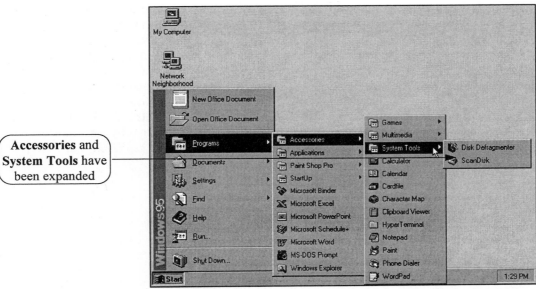

Accessories and **System Tools** have been expanded

Figure 2 - 2

3. To close the **Start** menu, click on the **Start** button again or on a blank part of the screen.

    REMEMBER: *Read the bulleted list that follows, but do not actually perform the steps until you reach Activity 2.1.*

To run a program from the Start menu:

- Click on the **Start** button.

- Point to **Programs**.

- Point to the listing for the program of your choice, or to a listing that will expand.

- When you are pointing to the program you want to run, click on the program name.

 NOTE: *Windows 3.1 users should remember that they no longer have to double-click on the program to get it to run; a single click now works.*

Activity 2.2: Running a Program from the Start Menu

1. Start *Windows 95*, if necessary.

 2. Click on the **Start** button.

 PROBLEM SOLVER: *If the Start button is not visible, point to the lower left corner of the screen and you will see it.*

3. Point to **Programs** (Figure 2-1).

   A panel that lists your installed programs will be displayed.

4. Move the mouse pointer to the next panel and point to **Accessories**.

   *The **Accessories** are a group of programs that come with Windows 95, including a calculator, Notepad, and other programs to help you organize and accomplish your tasks.*

5. Move to the mouse pointer to the next panel, move down the panel, and click on *WordPad* (see Figure 2-3).

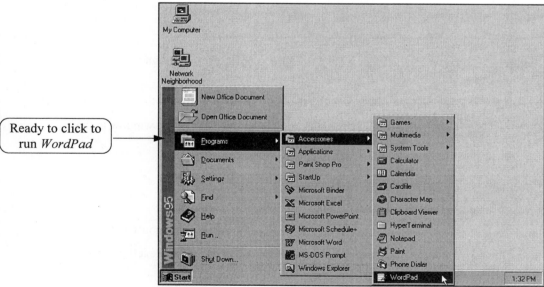

Figure 2 - 3

The WordPad program, one of the Windows 95 accessories, will open.

6. Close *WordPad* by clicking on its **Close** button.

7. Close any other windows that may have opened by accident.

8. Leave *Windows 95* open for the next activity.

NOTE: *Just as you can drag the mouse down a menu, you can also drag the mouse up from the Start button to Programs and across to the other columns. If you do, be careful, because as soon as you release the mouse button, the program you are pointing to will open.*

RUNNING MULTIPLE PROGRAMS

Unlike the *Windows 3.1* Program Manager, the Taskbar is always displayed (unless you have deliberately chosen to hide it). When you have run your first program, it is easy to return to the **Start** button and run another. The only limitation to the number of programs you can run is the capacity of your computer to hold the necessary instructions (the amount of RAM, or memory, installed on your computer).

Each program you run will open in its own window, at the size it was when last used. Sometimes the windows of different programs overlap or block each other. You will use the techniques we learned in Lesson 1 to move these windows aside and resize them when necessary. Windows may also be *Tiled* or *Cascaded* for maximum visibility, and you will practice these options too as you deal with a group of open windows on your Desktop.

Although many windows may be open simultaneously, only one program at a time may be *active*. If more than one window is open, only the active window will be affected by whatever action is taken next. The active window may be easily identified by its brightly colored Title Bar. To make an inactive window active, click on a part of the window that is showing, or click on the name of the window in the Taskbar. The Taskbar also differentiates between active windows (brightly colored button) and inactive windows (darker button).

To run multiple programs:

* Use the **Start** menu to open the first program as described above.

* Return to the **Start** menu and repeat the procedure to open other program(s).

To make a window active (if more than one window is open):

* Click on a part of the window that is visible, or click on the name of the window in the Taskbar.

To Cascade or Tile open windows:

* Click on an empty area of the Taskbar with the *right* mouse button.

* Click on **Cascade**, **Tile Horizontally**, or **Tile Vertically** with the *left* mouse button.

* To undo, click the *right* mouse button on the Taskbar again and click the left button on the command to undo the action you just performed.

To minimize all open windows:

* Click on an empty area of the Taskbar with the right mouse button.

* Click on **Minimize All Windows** with the left button.

Activity 2.3: Running Multiple Programs and Arranging them on the Desktop

1. Close any windows that are open on the Desktop.

2. Click on the **Start** button and point to **Programs**.

3. Point to **Accessories**.

4. At the Accessories panel, click on **Notepad**.

    The Notepad window will open. It may take a few seconds until it appears.

5. Repeat Steps 2 and 3, and then, instead of clicking on **Notepad**, click on **Character Map**.

6. Repeat the procedure and click on the **Clipboard Viewer** (sometimes called **Clipbook Viewer**).

7. Repeat the procedure and click on **Paint**.

8. Repeat the procedure and click on **WordPad**. Your screen should resemble Figure 2-4.

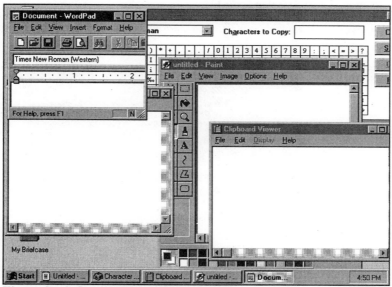

Figure 2 - 4 Overlapping Windows

PROBLEM SOLVER: *If any window opens at the maximized size, it will fill the entire screen and block all the other windows. To **Restore** (return a window to its previous size) a maximized window, click on its **Restore** button.*

When there are no maximized windows onscreen, you will see a group of overlapping windows of various sizes.

9. Drag the windows by their Title bars so that you can see as many at a time as possible (you should have opened a total of 5 windows).

    Remember that the Title Bar is the band at the top of the window containing its name. Notice how each window becomes active when you click on it. You can see the different color of the Title bar of the active window.

10. Click the *right mouse button* on an empty area of the Taskbar. The empty space may be as little as the space between buttons.

11. When the menu opens, click on **Cascade** with the *left* mouse button (see Figures 2-5 and 2-6).

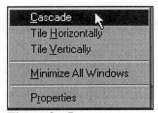

Figure 2 - 5

   PROBLEM SOLVER: *If you are not pointing within the Taskbar you will get a different menu when you click the right mouse button. Close that menu by clicking on a blank area of the Desktop and try again.*

12. Click on different Title bars in the cascade, and see how some windows become visible and others become blocked from view. Notice how you can still make a window active by clicking on part of it that is visible.

Once you have clicked on a Title bar, that window may block many others in the cascade.

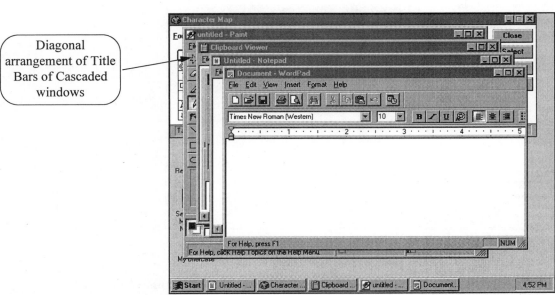

Diagonal arrangement of Title Bars of Cascaded windows

Figure 2 - 6 Cascaded Windows

13. To undo the cascade, click on a blank area of the Taskbar again with the *right mouse button* and choose **Undo Cascade** with the left mouse button.

14. Again, click the *right mouse button* on an empty area in the Taskbar.

15. Click on **Minimize all Windows**.

The windows disappear from the Desktop, but their names still appear on the Taskbar. Remember that although you cannot see the windows on the Desktop, they have not been closed. The minimized window's name on the Taskbar is the only sign that the window has not been closed.

16. Close each window in turn by clicking on its button on the Taskbar to Restore it as well as make it active, and then clicking on its **Close** button. Close any other windows that may have opened by accident.

17. Close any other windows that may have opened by accident.

    Remember that you may need to drag a window in order to make its Close button visible.

18. Leave *Windows 95* running for the next activity.

WHAT IS THE TASKBAR?

As you can see in Figure 2-1, the Taskbar contains the Start button and usually extends across the bottom of the screen. The Taskbar displays the names of all programs that are running, regardless of whether the windows are minimized or larger. Although the Taskbar's default position is across the bottom of the Desktop, you can change its location, size, and whether or not it is displayed.

To change the size of the Taskbar:

- Touch the top of the Taskbar with the mouse.

  The mouse appears as a double-headed arrow.

- Drag the top of the Taskbar up to increase its size.

- Drag the top of the Taskbar down to reduce its size.

To hide and unhide the Taskbar:

- Click the **Start** button and drag the mouse up to **Settings**, over and down to **Taskbar** and click.

- Click on the **Taskbar Options** index tab in the **Taskbar Properties** box.

- Click on **Auto hide** to place a check in that box and click on **OK**.

- To unhide the Taskbar, point to the **Start** button, repeat the procedure and remove the check from **Auto hide**.

  PROBLEM SOLVER: *If the Taskbar is still not visible, make sure that **Always on Top** is checked.*

To move the Taskbar:

- Click on an empty area of the Taskbar, and, while holding the mouse button down, drag the Taskbar to the top, left or right of the screen.

- Release the mouse button.

  The Taskbar will remain where you have dragged it.

Activity 2.4: Changing the Taskbar Settings

1. Close any windows that are open on the Desktop.

2. Click on the **Start** button.

3. Point to **Settings**, and then click on **Taskbar**.

4. To hide the Taskbar, click on the box in front of the words **Auto hide** to place a check in the box (see Figure 2-7).

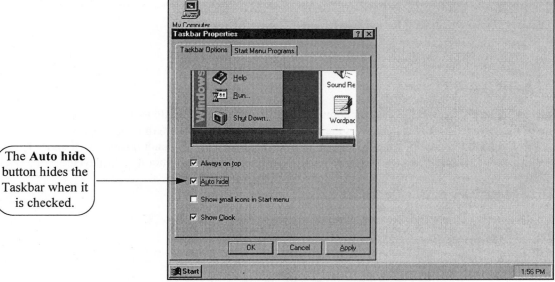

The **Auto hide** button hides the Taskbar when it is checked.

Figure 2 - 7 The Taskbar Properties Dialog Box

5. Click on **OK**.

   You will no longer be able to see the Taskbar.

6. To bring up the Taskbar, point anywhere along the bottom of the screen.

7. Move your mouse away from the bottom of the screen. What happens to the Taskbar?

8. Point to the bottom of the screen to bring up the Taskbar and click on the **Start** button.

9. Point to **Settings**, and then click on **Taskbar**.

10. To unhide the Taskbar, remove the check by clicking again on the box in front of **Auto hide**.

11. Click on **OK**.

 PROBLEM SOLVER: *If the Taskbar is still not visible, make sure that **Always on Top** is checked on the **Taskbar Options** tab of the **Taskbar Properties** box.*

12. To enlarge the Taskbar, point anywhere along the *top* of the Taskbar.

    Your cursor will change to a double-headed arrow.

13. Drag the mouse up and release the mouse button.

14. Drag again to return the Taskbar to its original height.

15. Click the mouse inside the Taskbar and drag it to the top of your screen. Make sure the mouse pointer looks like a single-headed arrow when you do this.

16. Release the mouse button.

17. Drag your Taskbar to either the left or right side of the screen and release the mouse button (see Figure 2-8).

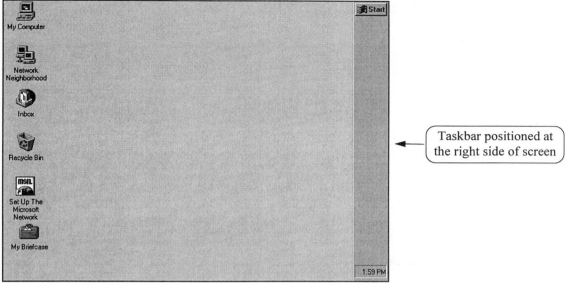

Taskbar positioned at the right side of screen

Figure 2 - 8

18. Return the Taskbar to its original location.

19. Leave *Windows 95* open for the next activity.

LOOKING AT A TYPICAL WINDOW

In the next part of the Lesson 2, you will take another look at a typical window and its elements, using as an example, the WordPad program. Because these *Windows* elements appear in almost all windows, you will be able to recognize them in windows you have never seen before. Figure 2-9 displays the elements of a typical window. You have already worked with most of these elements.

Every window contains a small icon in its upper left corner which contains the **Control Menu**. Each window has a distinctive icon, but every **Control menu** is the same. In WordPad, for example, the **Control menu** icon looks like a document. The **Control menu** lets you control the size and placement of a window, as well as whether it is open or closed. You have already learned other methods for doing these procedures.

The **Control menu** is found to the left of the **Title Bar**. The Title bar of a window contains the name of the program, as well as the name of the current document, if there is one. To the right of the Title bar are the three buttons you worked with in Lesson 1, the **Minimize**, **Maximize/Restore** and **Close** buttons. The Minimize button removes the window from the Desktop but keeps its name on the Taskbar. The Maximize button enlarges the window so that it fills the entire screen.

When a window is maximized, the Maximize button becomes the Restore button. Clicking on the Restore button returns the window to its previous size. The Close button closes the window.

Below the Title bar, a typical window may or may not contain a **Menu Bar**, (horizontal list of menu words as described in Lesson 1), and below the Menu Bar there may be one or more **Toolbars** (rows of buttons used to perform important tasks). Each window is bordered by a four-sided window frame.

A window may also contain horizontal and/or vertical scroll arrows (not pictured) that let you move to parts of the document that do not fit on the current screen.

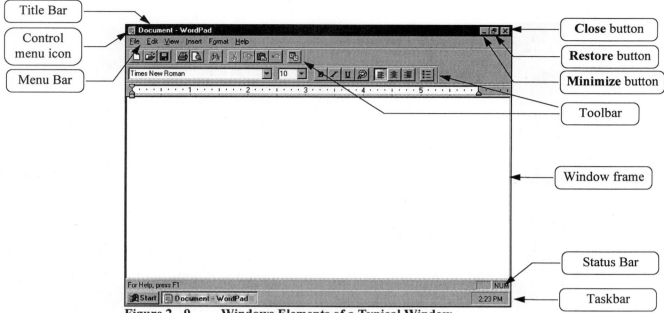

Figure 2 - 9   Windows Elements of a Typical Window

Activity 2.5: Entering Text

In this activity you will begin to practice *Windows 95* basics by opening WordPad and entering some text. You will learn a great deal more about WordPad in Lesson 5.

1.   To open WordPad, click on the **Start** button, point to **Programs**, then **Accessories**, and then click on **WordPad**.

      The WordPad window will open.

2.   Maximize the WordPad screen.

      It is a good idea to maximize a word processing application, so that you have as much workspace as possible.

3.   Look at Figure 2-9 and match the parts of the window in the picture with the same parts on your screen.

      PROBLEM SOLVER: *If your screen does not show the WordPad Toolbar, click on the **View** menu and click on **Toolbar**. If other elements pictured in Figure 2-9 are missing from your screen, do not worry. You will learn to display them in Lesson 5.*

4.   Type your name and press **ENTER**.

      *If you make any mistakes while typing, use the **BACKSPACE** key to erase them and then type correctly.*

5.   Type your address, pressing **ENTER** after each line.

6.   Leave WordPad running for the next activity.

BASIC WINDOWS TASKS

In the *Windows* environment, one of the biggest plusses is that once you have learned to begin a new document, open, save, and print it, you will do those procedures in exactly the same way in all *Windows* programs. This consistency, plus the similar appearance of all windows makes it faster and easier to learn new programs.

In the next part of Lesson 2, you will learn to begin, save, open, and print files in WordPad. Once you have completed these tasks, you will be able to repeat them in any *Windows* program.

To begin a new document:

- Click on **FILE/New** at the menu, or click the **New** button on the Toolbar.

  *If the toolbar is not visible, click on **VIEW/Toolbar**.*

  *A dialog box may appear asking for more information about the type of file you want to create. If so, select the file type and then click on **OK**.*

  *Sometimes, you will be asked whether you want to Save Changes to the current document. Answer **Yes** or **No**. If the document has a name, the changes will be saved and a blank document will appear. If the document you are trying to save does not have a name, the **Save As** dialog box will appear (see **Save As**, below).*

To open a document:

- Click on **FILE/Open** at the menu, or click the **Open** button on the Toolbar.
- If necessary, open the **Look in:** box and click on the folder that contains the document you want to open.
- If necessary, open the **Files of type:** box and click on the type of file you want to open.
- Click on the name of the file you want to open.
- Click on **OK** or press **ENTER**.

To save a document for the first time:

- Click on **FILE/Save As** at the menu, or click the **Save** button on the toolbar.
- Type a name for the document. You may use any name you like. In *Windows 95* you are no longer limited to 8 characters, and you are no longer prohibited from using spaces within the file name. You may now use up to 250 characters in the file name. Examples of *Windows 95* file names not acceptable in *DOS* or *Windows 3.11*:

  mortgage letter   cover letter to abc corp   2nd reminder notice to intech labs

- Pick a place to store your file from the **Save in:** list at the top of the dialog box. You may save the file directly to the Desktop, to a floppy drive, hard drive, or network drive.
- Double-click on the folder in which you wish to save the file.

  A folder (also called a directory) is an area on a disk where the document will be saved. All the documents in a folder have a logical reason for being saved in the same place, for example being the same type of document, or being created by the same application. You will learn about creating folders and organizing documents in Lesson 7.

- If you would like to create a new folder first and then save your file in it, click on the **Create New Folder** button. Type the name of the new folder and press **ENTER**. Then, double-click on the folder you just created.
- Select the *type* of file to be saved.

  Most of the time, you will leave this part of the dialog box alone. Changing the file type allows you to save a file in a form that can be used by another program. For example, you could create a document using Word for Windows and save it as a WordPerfect for Windows document.

- Click on **OK** or press **ENTER**.

To save a document that already has a name:

- Click on **FILE/Save** at the menu, or click the **Save** button on the toolbar.

The file will be re-saved. The current version of the document will be saved in place of the old version. After this has been done, there is no way to get the old version back.

To save a document while giving it a new name:

- Follow the directions above for saving a file for the first time, except that you *must* choose **FILE/Save As** at the menu. Do *not* click the **Save** button on the toolbar—this will resave your file keeping the same name.

To print a document:

- Make sure your printer is turned on and that it contains paper.
- Click on **FILE/Print** at the menu.
- Click on **OK** when you have made your choices at the dialog box.

  ALTERNATE: *Click on the **Print** button* *on the toolbar to print a single copy of the document that is on your screen.*

Activity 2.6: Practicing Basic Windows Tasks: Saving, Printing, Closing

As you begin this activity, *WordPad* should be running and your name and address should be typed onscreen. If not, repeat Activity 2.5.

1. Insert your formatted 3 ½" data disk into the floppy disk drive on your computer.

   *In order to proceed, you will need to know the letter name of the drive that contains your data disk (probably **a:**). If you do not know, ask your instructor or lab assistant.*

2. To save the document containing your name and address, at the menu click on **FILE/Save As** or click on the **Save** button.

   *The **Save As** dialog box will open (see Figure 2-10). The word **Document** in the **File Name** box is highlighted, indicating that this part of the dialog box is currently active. **Document** is a temporary name. You will type the permanent name for the document in that space.*

3. Type the following file name: **first windows95 file**. Do not type the period after the file name.

   Windows 3.1 users will quickly notice that the file name has more than 8 characters and contains 2 spaces. This is not a problem, because long file names are now accepted in Windows 95.

   PROBLEM SOLVER: *If you have moved to another part of the dialog box, the word **Document** will not be highlighted. Drag over the word to highlight it and type the file name.*

4. To save the file on the floppy drive, open the list next to the **Save in:** box, and click on the picture of the floppy drive containing your data disk.

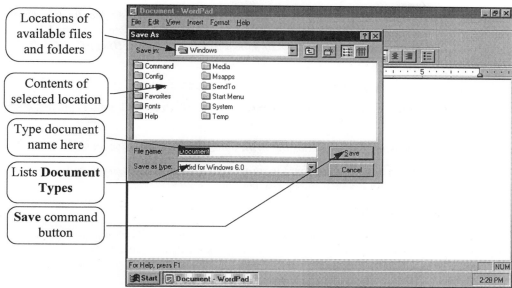

Locations of available files and folders

Contents of selected location

Type document name here

Lists Document Types

Save command button

Figure 2 - 10   The Save As Dialog Box

 PROBLEM SOLVER: *If you are using an unformatted disk, you will see an error message on your screen. You cannot save documents on an unformatted disk. To format the disk, follow the instructions in Appendix 1, or switch to a formatted disk.*

5. Make sure that the box next to **Save as type:** reads **Word for Windows 6.0**.

    *If not, open the list and click on **Word for Windows 6.0**.*

6. Click on the **Save** command button. An hourglass will appear as the document is saved and will disappear when saving is complete.

    *The dialog box will close. The document name you typed (**first windows95 file**) will appear on the Title Bar of WordPad and on the Taskbar (see Figure 2-11).*

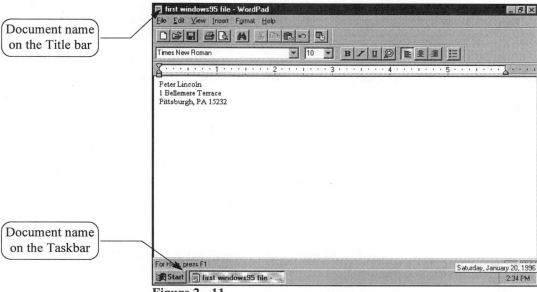

Document name on the Title bar

Document name on the Taskbar

Figure 2 - 11

PROBLEM SOLVER: *If your Title Bar reads: first windows95 file.doc, the file extensions are being shown. If you want to hide them, open the My Computer window, open the View menu, click on Options, the View index tab, and the check box marked: Hide MS-DOS file extensions...*

7. Make sure your printer is turned on and that it contains paper.

8. To print your file, click on **FILE/Print** at the menu. When the **Print** dialog box appears, click on **OK**.

   If your toolbar is showing, you may click the Print button to print your document.

9. Use the gray arrow keys on your keyboard to move your blinking cursor to the end of the last line of your address. Press **ENTER** to begin a new line.

10. Add your telephone number to the bottom of your document on a separate line.

   Now the version of the file that you saved is no longer accurate—it does not contain your telephone number. We will resave the document, keeping the same name. The old version of the file will be replaced by the current version, which will include your telephone number.

11. To resave the file, click on **FILE/Save** at the menu.

   No dialog box will open, but if you glance at the Status Bar you can see a message telling you that the file is being saved.

12. Print the document again.

13. To close WordPad, click on its **Close** button.

14. Leave *Windows 95* running for the next activity.

CREATING A DATA DISK

In order to continue using this book, you will need to have more documents saved on your data disk. You will use them as "dummy" documents—files you can use for practice, but which contain nothing of importance. You will return to some of these documents in later lessons as you learn to copy, move and delete files. In the next activity, you will add documents to your data disk for this purpose. Even though the documents you create will each contain only a few words, you may use them just as you would any other file.

Activity 2.7: Opening a Document and Adding to Your Data Disk

In this activity, you practice opening a document. Then, you will save a number of small documents on your data disk to use as you work through the rest of this book.

1. Turn on your computer, if it is not already on.

2. Make sure the disk you used in the last activity is inserted into your floppy drive.

3. To open WordPad, click the **Start** button, point to **Programs** and then to **Accessories**.

4. Click on **WordPad**.

   If the Toolbar is not displayed, click on the View menu and click on Toolbar.

5. To open the document you saved in the last activity, click on **FILE/Open** or click on the **Open** button on the Toolbar.

6. Open the **Look in:** box by clicking on the ↓ and click on the drive containing your data disk.

7. Click on the listing for: **first windows95 file** (see Figure 2-12).

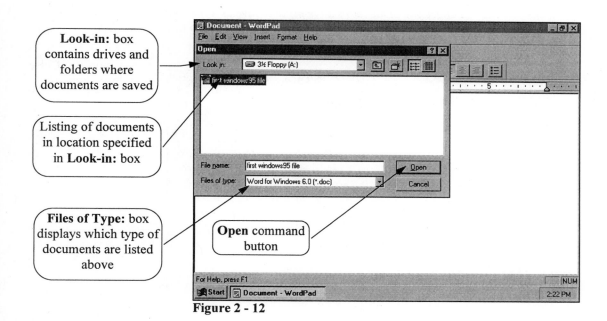

Look-in: box contains drives and folders where documents are saved

Listing of documents in location specified in Look-in: box

Files of Type: box displays which type of documents are listed above

Open command button

Figure 2 - 12

 PROBLEM SOLVER: *If the file is not listed, open the **Files of Type** box and click on **All Documents**. You should see the file name listed and should click on it. If not, you have not followed Step 5 correctly, or you did not save the file in Activity 2.3.*

8. Click on the **Open** command button.

9. Examine the document.

    This is indeed the file you saved in the last activity. Now you will begin a new file.

10. At the Menu Bar, choose **FILE/New**.

11. If you are asked what type of file you want to begin, make sure **Word 6.0 Document** is selected and click on **OK.**

12. On the blank screen, type: **This is a test document**.

13. Choose **FILE/Save As** to save the document. The floppy drive will come up automatically because you switched to it earlier in this activity.

 PROBLEM SOLVER: *If for some reason the **Save in:** box does not contain the floppy drive name, click the ↓ to the right of the location currently listed and click on the name of the drive containing your data disk.*

14. Type: **test document 1** as the document name.

15. Leave the file type as **Word for Windows 6.0.**

16. Click on the gray **Save** command button to save the file.

17. To begin a new document, at the Menu Bar, click on **FILE/New**.

18. Make sure **Word 6.0 Document** is selected and click on **OK.**

19. Repeat Steps 12 - 18 to save another document on your data disk. Then, repeat Steps 10-18 to save 4 more documents. As document names, use **test document 2, test document 3**, etc. Save a few words as the contents of each file. Your last document will be **test document 6**.

*Notice that any changes you made to the **Save in:** and **Save as Type:** boxes will remain. You only need to type the new file name and click the **Save** button. When you save the last document, the **Save As** box should resemble Figure 2-13.*

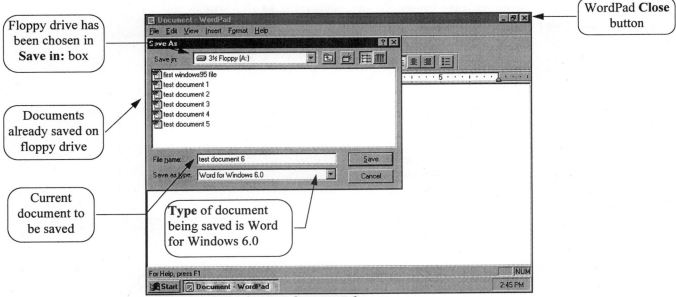

Figure 2 - 13 Saving test document 6

20. After all the documents have been saved on your data disk click on the **Close** button to close WordPad.

21. To see the documents you created listed elsewhere in *Windows 95*, at the Desktop, double-click on **My Computer**.

22. Double-click on the listing for the floppy drive that contains your data disk (see Figure 2-14).

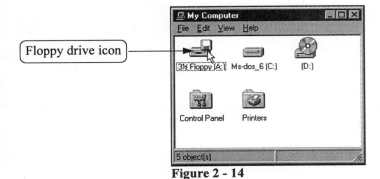

Figure 2 - 14

*You should see an icon representing each document you saved with its name beneath it (see Figure 2-15). If your screen does not match the figure, click on **VIEW/Large icons**.*

PROBLEM SOLVER: *If your Title Bar does not include the words: 3 1/2 Floppy, you may change this by clicking on **VIEW/Options**, clicking on the **View** index tab, and removing the check from the box that reads: **Display the full MS-DOS path in the title bar**.*

23. Close the **My Computer** window and the floppy drive window.

24. Remove your disk from the floppy disk drive, and label it: **Data disk for Getting Started with *Windows 95***. Include your name on the label. Do not lose the disk!

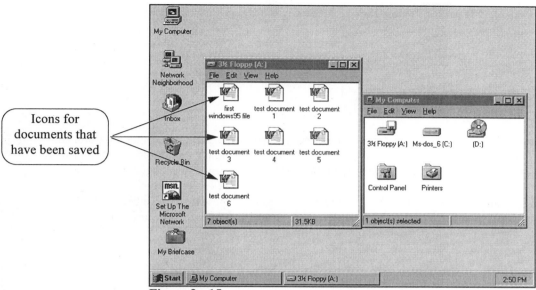

Figure 2 - 15

25. Shut down *Windows 95*.

WHAT IS THE WINDOWS 95 CLIPBOARD?

The *Windows 95* Clipboard (sometimes called the Clipbook) is a location used for temporary storage during the transfer of data from one location to another. Only one set of data at a time may occupy the Clipboard.

Data is automatically sent to the Clipboard during a Copy or Move procedure. You may also place data in the Clipboard by pressing the **PRINTSCREEN** key. This allows you to place an image of your current screen in the Clipboard. You may then paste the image into WordPad, or another word processor, and print it.

We will use the Clipboard in many of the Independent Projects. It will enable you to print what is on your screen as you follow the instructions within a project. The following activity will teach you to use the Clipboard for this purpose.

Activity 2.8: Using the Clipboard to Capture a Screen Image

1. Turn on your computer.

2. Run the **Calculator** program (it is one of the Accessories).

3. Press the **PRINTSCREEN** key.

   PRINTSCREEN is a gray key which is found on the topmost row of your keyboard to the right of the function keys (F1 - F12). Pressing PRINTSCREEN copies the contents of your screen to the Clipboard.

   Now we will transfer that image to a WordPad document and print it.

4. Run WordPad.

5. To place the image into WordPad, at the Menu Bar, click on **EDIT/Paste**.

   The image you copied to the Clipboard will be pasted into the WordPad document. You will need to scroll up to see the image.

6. To print the document, click on **FILE/Print** and **OK**.

7. Click on **FILE/Exit** to close the WordPad window. Answer **No** when you are asked if you want to save changes to your document.

8. Close the Calculator.

9. Shut down *Windows 95*.

SUMMARY

In Lesson 2 you learned to use the Start menu to run programs. You ran a single program, and then several programs from the Start menu, and learned to handle the multiple open windows of those programs. You became familiar with the Taskbar and learned to changed its size and position. As you learned to perform basic tasks in the *Windows 95* environment (creating, saving, opening, and printing documents), you understood that once these tasks have been learned they can be performed in the same way in all *Windows* programs. Finally, you learned to copy an image to the Clipboard and paste it into a WordPad document.

KEY TERMS

Accessories	FILE/New	Printscreen
Auto hide	FILE/Print	Programs
Cascade	FILE/Save	Restore button
Clipboard	FILE/Save As	Start menu
Close button	Maximize button	Taskbar
Control menu	Menu bar	Tile
Create new folder	Minimize button	Title bar
Dialog box	Notepad	Toolbar
File name	Paint	WordPad

INDEPENDENT PROJECTS

The independent projects for Lesson 2 will help you practice the skills introduced in the lesson as well as learn new skills. You will see that instructions for the projects are not as detailed as instructions for the activities in the lesson. You should be able to draw upon the skills you have learned and work independently to complete the projects. If you are unable to complete the projects, re-do the lesson activities for further practice and then try the independent projects again.

Independent Project 2.1: Using Multiple Programs

1. Turn on your computer, if it is not already on.

2. Insert your data disk into the floppy drive.

3. Run the following programs from the Start menu: *Calculator, Character Map, Clipboard Viewer, Notepad, Paint, WordPad, Minesweeper, Solitaire*. All these programs are Accessories, except for Solitaire and Minesweeper, which are games.

 PROBLEM SOLVER: *If any of the windows opens maximized (covering the entire screen), click on its Restore button.*

4. Expand the Taskbar (make it taller) so that you can see the full names of all the programs you have opened.

5. **Tile** the programs vertically.

6. Make the calculator active by clicking on its window.

7. Click on the numbers: **210**. You may need to move the Calculator.

8. Click on the * on the calculator.

9. Click on the numbers: **84**

10. Click on the = on the calculator.

    You should see the number 17640 as your answer.

11. Press the **PRINTSCREEN** key.

12. Make WordPad active by clicking on its button on the Taskbar. The WordPad button may be small enough so that all you see of it is the word **Document**.

13. Click on **EDIT/Paste** to paste the Calculator image into WordPad.

14. Print the image by clicking on **FILE/Print** and **OK**.

15. Click on the calculator button on the Taskbar to make it active again.

16. Close the calculator.

17. Make **Solitaire** the active window.

18. Use the **GAME/Deck** command to change the picture on the card backs. Choose the pattern you like best.

19. Close **Solitaire**.

20. **Cascade** the remaining applications.

    This will not work properly if the Taskbar is too tall. If necessary, drag the top down a bit.

21. Make WordPad active by clicking on its name on the Taskbar.

22. Begin a new WordPad document. Do not save changes to the last document.

23. On the WordPad screen, type a list of the courses you are taking this semester, pressing **ENTER** after each course name. Press **ENTER** again and type your name.

24. Save the file on your data disk as **current courses**. Remember to make sure the **Save in:** box indicates the drive containing your data disk.

25. Print the file.

26. Close *WordPad*. If you are asked if you wish to save changes, answer **No**.

27. Minimize all the remaining windows except for Minesweeper.

    Minesweeper is now the only window that is not minimized. Look at the Taskbar and notice the difference between how Minesweeper (the active applications) is listed compared to the applications that are minimized. The active application is listed in white on the Taskbar.

28. Minimize *Minesweeper*.

29. To close the windows, click the *right mouse button* on the listing for each of the minimized programs at the Taskbar and then click on **Close** to close each window. No windows should remain open on the Desktop.

30. Return the Taskbar to its previous size.

31. Shut down *Windows 95*.

Independent Project 2.2: Practicing Basic Tasks

In this activity we will use WordPad to practice tasks you learned in Lesson 2, to learn Toolbar shortcuts, and how to insert dates and bullets.

1. Turn on your computer, if it is not already on.

2. Insert your data disk into the floppy drive.

3. Run WordPad.

4. Maximize the WordPad window, if it is not already maximized.

5. Click on the **View** menu and make sure there are checks next to **Toolbar, Format Bar, Ruler** and **Status Bar**. If any of these items *is not checked,* click on it.

6. At the Menu Bar, click on **INSERT/Date and Time**.

7. At the **Date and Time** box, click on the time/date format of your choice.

8. Click on **OK**.

   The current date will be placed in your document.

9. Press **ENTER** twice.

10. Type a short paragraph describing possible tasks for which you might use *WordPad*. Do not press **ENTER** while you are typing the paragraph. If you make a mistake, press the **BACKSPACE** key and retype.

11. After you have finished typing the paragraph, press **ENTER** twice and type your name, Student ID number, and any other required information. Put this information on each document you print from now on.

12. To save the document, click on the **Save** button on the Toolbar.

    *This is an alternative to using the **FILE/Save As** command at the menu.*

13. Save the document on your data disk using the directions given to you earlier in the lesson. Type the following filename: **uses for WordPad**

14. To print the document, click on the **Print** button on the Toolbar.

    This is an alternative to use the FILE/Print command at the menu.

15. To begin a new document, click on the **New** button on the Toolbar.

    This is an alternative to use the FILE/New command at the menu.

    If you are asked if you wish to save changes, answer No.

16. Click on **Word 6.0 Document** and **OK**.

17. To insert the date, click on the **Date/Time** button on the Toolbar and click on **OK**.

    *This is an alternative to use the **INSERT/Date and Time** command at the menu.*

18. Press **ENTER**.

19. Type your name and ID and press **ENTER** again.

20. Click on the Bullet button to turn on the bulleted list feature.

21. Type a short list of things you would like to learn to do at the computer. Press **ENTER** after each one to begin a new line and get a new bullet.

    You will see a bullet for each item you type.

22. Save the document on your data disk with the name **computer goals for this semester**.

23. Print the document.

24. Close WordPad.

25. Shut down *Windows 95*.

Independent Project 2.3: Applying Basic Skills to Paint

In this activity, you will explore a new program, Paint, using the skills you have learned.

1. Turn on your computer, if it is not already on.

2. Insert your data disk into the floppy drive.

3. From the Start menu, open the Paint program. It is listed under Accessories.

4. Click on the **View** menu and make sure there is a check mark in front of the words: **Tool Box**. If there is *no check*, click on the words.

   The Tool box is the double row of buttons to the left of the Paint workspace.

5. Click on the **View** menu again, and make sure there is a check mark in front of the words: **Color Box**. If there is *no check*, click on the words.

   The Color Box is the double row of colors under the workspace.

6. On the Tool Box, point to the button picturing the rectangle and click on it.

7. Move the mouse onto the workspace, click and drag to the right to draw a rectangle.

   Notice the new shape of the mouse pointer.

8. To change the color of the next figure you draw, click on a different color from the Color Box.

9. At the Tool Box, click on a different shape and experiment with it on the workspace.

10. Choose **FILE/New** to begin a new document.

11. Answer **No** when you are asked if you want to save changes.

12. At the new document screen, choose a color from the Color Box and at the Tool Box, click on the Pencil button.

13. Write your name with the mouse in script by holding down the left mouse button and dragging to write on the workspace. It will not be easy to do. Don't forget to dot your i's and cross your t's.

14. Experiment with decorating your name using the various tools. If you draw something you don't like, click on **EDIT/Undo** at the Menu Bar to remove it.

15. Save the document on your data disk as: **first paint file**. Change the **Save as type:** listing from **256 Color Bitmap** to **16 Color Bitmap**. This will keep the file size small and prevent the data disk from filling up.

16. Print the document using **FILE/Print**.

   Remember that the file will print in black and white unless you have a color printer.

17. Begin another new file by clicking on **FILE/New**.

18. Create a drawing that has at least 3 shapes and 3 different colors.

19. Save the file on your data disk as **second paint file**. Again, the file type must be **16 Color Bitmap**.

20. Print the file.

21. Close the **Paint** program.

22. Shut down *Windows 95*.

Lesson

3 Using the Control Panel

Objectives

In this lesson you will learn how to:

- Understand the functions managed by the Control Panel
- Customize the Desktop
- Change the background of the Desktop

- Change the appearance of the Desktop
- Use the screen saver
- Adjust the mouse
- Change the date and time

WHAT IS THE CONTROL PANEL?

The *Control Panel* is the place where you can make *Windows 95* "look and feel" the way you want. It is the window that contains programs that let you set and keep your own preferences for *Windows 95*. At the Control Panel, you can change the color and pattern of your screen, add or remove hardware and software, set up your computer to send and receive faxes, and set your mouse to move and click at the speed you like best.

In this lesson, you will use several of the Control Panel programs. You will change the background and appearance of the *Windows 95* Desktop. You will change and use several of the available screen savers. Then, you will change the settings for the mouse to suit your preferences. Finally, you will change the date and time for your computer.

	Control Panel Program	Description
	Accessibility Options	For users who find the PC difficult to see or control; this option lets you change keyboard, sound, display, and mouse settings so that they are easier to use.
	Add New Hardware	This option guides you through installation of a new piece of hardware.
	Add/Remove Programs	This option guides you through the installation or removal of software.
	Date/Time	With this option, you can set the date, time, and time zone for your system. You can choose to automatically adjust the time for Daylight Saving Time.
	Display	This option lets you change the colors, patterns, and wallpaper for the desktop. You can also select a screen saver and adjust the color palette.
	Fonts	You can install, remove, or view fonts with this option.
	Keyboard	The Keyboard option allows you to adjust the speed of the character repeat and the cursor blink rate. You can also change the installed language or the keyboard type.
	Mail and Fax	This option sets up profiles for sending e-mail and faxes.
	Microsoft Mail Postoffice	You can set up Microsoft Mail with this option.
	Modems	With this option you can set up or remove modems.
	Mouse	Use this option to change the mouse to left-handed settings, change the double-click speed, change the appearance of the pointers, add mouse trails, or change the mouse type.
	Multimedia	This option is used to set up audio, MIDI, CD Music, and advanced multimedia properties of your computer system.
	Network	With this option, you can set up network access, including configuration and identification.
	ODBC	Use this option to add, remove, or configure data sources.
	Passwords	You can add or change *Windows* passwords with this option.
	Printers	Add or remove printers with this option.
	Regional Settings	Use this option to set expressions for numbers, currency, time, and date in various regions of the world.
	Sounds	You can select sounds for various *Windows* actions with this option.
	System	With this option, you can display your registration number, type of PC, and amount of available Random Access Memory.

Table 3 - 1

REMEMBER: *Read the bulleted list that follows, but do not actually perform the steps until you reach Activity 3.1.*

To open the Control Panel window:

- Click on the **Start** button.

  A menu will appear above the Taskbar.

- Point to **Settings**, and click on **Control Panel**.

  The Control Panel window appears.

Activity 3.1: Opening the Control Panel Window

In this activity you will open the Control Panel window.

1. Click on the **Start** button.

   A menu appears above the Taskbar (see Figure 3-1).

Figure 3 - 1

2. Point to **SETTINGS**, and then click on **Control Panel**.

   The Control Panel window appears on the screen (see Figure 3-2).

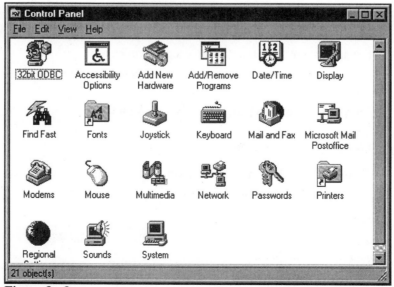

Figure 3 - 2

3. If necessary, maximize the Control Panel window so that you can see all the icons.

4. Leave the Control Panel open for the next activity.

CUSTOMIZING THE DESKTOP

Since no two people have exactly the same tastes, *Windows 95* can be customized so that its settings reflect the preferences of each user. One of the most common features to customize is the Desktop. The icon that controls the appearance of the Desktop is the Display icon. When opened, the Display window has panels: Background, Screen Saver, Appearance, and Settings. The **Background** panel allows you to change the color and pattern of the Desktop. The **Screen Saver** panel lets you select the moving image that protects the monitor when the computer is not used for a set period of time. The **Appearance** panel allows you to choose a color scheme for *Windows 95* that is appealing to you. You can also create and save your own color scheme if you like. The **Settings** panel lets you set the number of colors on the color palette and the size of the Desktop.

In the next part of Lesson 3, you will customize your Desktop by changing the background, appearance, and screen saver.

Changing the Background of the Desktop

The **Background** panel allows you to change either the *pattern* or the *wallpaper* for the Desktop. A pattern is a small, repeated design that gives a textured look to the Desktop. A wallpaper design is brighter and bolder. Only one of these options should be selected. If you decide to "wallpaper" your Desktop, you may either *Tile* the pattern so that the whole Desktop is covered, or you may *Center* the pattern so that one copy of the pattern will be placed in the middle of the Desktop.

To select a pattern for the background:

*   Click on the **Start** button on the Taskbar.

*   Point to **Settings** and click on **Control Panel**.

*   Double-click on the **Display** icon   .

    The Display Properties window appears on the screen. The four index tabs appearing below the Title Bar will open the four panels. Any of these index tabs may be showing as the window is displayed.

*   Click on the **Background** index tab.

*   Choose **(None)** in the **Wallpaper** drop-down list box.

*   Select any pattern from the **Pattern** drop-down list box.

    As you select patterns, they will be displayed in the sample screen in the top portion of the Display Properties window.

*   When you have found a pattern you like, click on **OK**.

To select wallpaper for the background:

*   Click on the **Start** button on the Taskbar.

*   Point to **Settings** and click on **Control Panel**.

*   Double-click on the **Display** icon   .

    The Display Properties window appears on the screen (see Figure 3-3). The four index tabs appear below the Title Bar.

*   Click on the **Background** tab, if necessary.

*   Choose **(None)** in the **Pattern** drop-down list box.

- Select any wallpaper from the **Wallpaper** drop-down list box.

  As you try different wallpaper selections, they will be displayed in the sample screen in the top portion of the Display Properties window.

- Click on either the **Center** or the **Tile** button.

  *When you select the **Center** button, the wallpaper is displayed once in the center of the sample screen. When you select **Tile**, the wallpaper pattern is repeated across the background of the screen.*

- When you find a wallpaper selection you like, click on **OK**.

  NOTE: *If both a wallpaper and a pattern are chosen and the wallpaper is tiled, only the wallpaper will be displayed.*

Activity 3.2: Changing the Background of the Desktop

In this activity, you will change the background of your Desktop using both the Pattern and the Wallpaper options.

1. After Activity 3.1, the Control Panel window should be open and maximized. If the Control Panel window is not showing on the screen, select **SETTINGS/Control Panel** from the **Start** menu.

2. Double-click on the **Display** icon.

  *The Display Properties window appears on the screen. The four index tabs appear below the Title Bar. Any of these tabs may be showing as the window is displayed. In Figure 3-3, the **Background** tab is showing.*

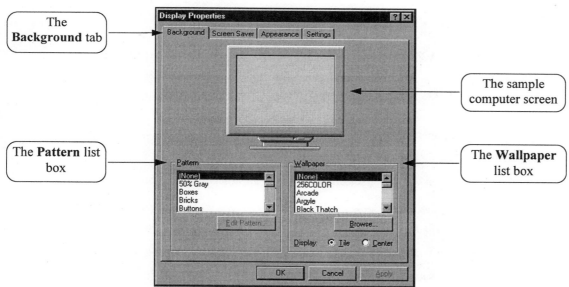

Figure 3 - 3

3. Click on the **Background** index tab, if necessary.

  *The **Background** panel appears on the screen. A sample computer screen is showing at the top of the window. This computer screen will illustrate the selected backgrounds. The **Pattern** and **Wallpaper** list boxes appear below the sample computer screen (see Figure 3-3). The sample computer will not show both a pattern and a wallpaper selection unless the wallpaper selection is centered. So that you can see the full effect of both the patterns and the wallpaper selections, you will select **(None)** in the list box of the item you are not currently looking at.*

4. Write down the current Pattern and Wallpaper selections so that you will be able to change back to the original settings later in this lesson.

5. Select **(None)** in the **Wallpaper** list box, if it is not the current choice.

6. To view the available patterns, select a pattern from the **Pattern** list box.

   The pattern should appear in the sample computer screen.

 PROBLEM SOLVER: *If the sample screen turns black even though you have a color scheme selected, click on the **Appearance** index tab; click on the* ↓ *to open the list below the word, **Scheme**; scroll to the bottom of the list and select **Windows (Standard)** color scheme, and then click on **Apply**. Then, click on the **Background** index tab and select the pattern again.*

7. Continue clicking on patterns in the **Pattern** list box until you see one you like.

8. Click on **OK**.

   The Control Panel window should still be maximized, blocking your view of the pattern.

9. Minimize the Control Panel window and take a look at the pattern you chose.

   The pattern will appear on the background of the Desktop using the previously selected background color. You will select a color scheme later in this lesson.

10. Click on the **Control Panel** button on the Taskbar to return the window to its previous size.

11. Double-click on the **Display** icon.

    *When the Display Properties window appears on the screen, the **Background panel** should still be showing.*

12. To remove the pattern, click on **(None)** in the **Pattern** list box.

 PROBLEM SOLVER: *(None) is the first item in the list; if necessary, scroll up until it is displayed.*

13. To cover your Desktop with wallpaper, click on the **Tile** button below the **Wallpaper** list box.

14. To choose a wallpaper, click on a wallpaper name in the **Wallpaper** list box.

    The wallpaper should appear on the sample computer screen.

15. Continue clicking on wallpaper selections on the **Wallpaper** list until you see one you like.

16. Click on **OK**.

    You will return to the Desktop. The Control Panel window should still be maximized.

17. Minimize the Control Panel window so you can see the wallpaper you chose.

    Do you like the pattern you picked?

18. Click on the **Control Panel** button on the Taskbar to return the window to its previous size.

19. Leave the Control Panel window open for the next activity.

Changing the Appearance of the Desktop

The **Appearance** panel allows you to change the color scheme of the Desktop. *Windows 95* ships with approximately 20 color schemes, some of which have larger text to make it easier to read the screen. You can also customize a color scheme if you wish.

To select a color scheme:

- Click on the **Start** button on the Taskbar.

- Point to **Settings** and click on **Control Panel**.

- Double-click on the **Display** icon .

  The Display Properties window appears on the screen.

- Click on the **Appearance** index tab.

- Choose a color scheme from the **Scheme** drop-down list box.

  The selected scheme will appear in the top preview area of the window.

- Click on **OK**.

  You will return to the Desktop.

To change single elements of the color scheme:

- Click on the **Start** button on the Taskbar.

- Point to **Settings** and click on **Control Panel**.

- Double-click on the **Display** icon .

  The Display Properties window appears on the screen.

- Click on the **Appearance** index tab.

- Choose the item you wish to change from the **Item** drop-down list box.

  *If the item has text elements, the **Font** list box will be activated and you can make font, font size, font color, and font attribute changes. If the item does not have text elements, you will only be able to change the size and color of the item.*

- Choose your selections from the various options.

- Click on **OK**.

  You will return to the Desktop.

Activity 3.3: Changing the Color Scheme of the Desktop

In this activity, you will select a color scheme that *Windows 95* has provided. You will also customize the color scheme to suit your needs.

1. After Activity 3.2, the Control Panel window should still be open and maximized. If it is not, select **SETTINGS/Control Panel** from the **Start** menu.

2. Double-click on the **Display** icon.

    The Display Properties window appears on the screen.

3. Click on the **Appearance** index tab.

    *The **Appearance** panel appears in the Display Properties window as shown in Figure 3-4. You will select a preset color scheme first.*

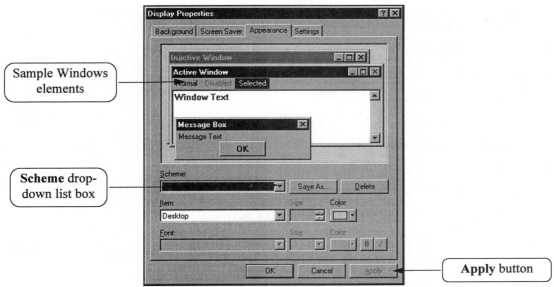

Figure 3 - 4

4. Write down the current color scheme so that you can change it back later in this lesson.

5. Click the ↓ to open the list under the word, **Scheme** (Figure 3-4), and then click on the **Brick** color scheme in the **Scheme** drop-down list box.

PROBLEM SOLVER: *If you do not see **Brick**, scroll up until it is visible.*

The color scheme of the sample Windows elements will change in the top of the dialog box.

5. Continue clicking on selections until you have seen all of the available color schemes. After you have seen the available color schemes, click on **Eggplant**.

6. Click on the **Apply** button in the lower right corner of the window.

*The Eggplant color scheme is applied to the current open windows on the Desktop, and the **Appearance** tab stays on-screen. Now you will change several of the options.*

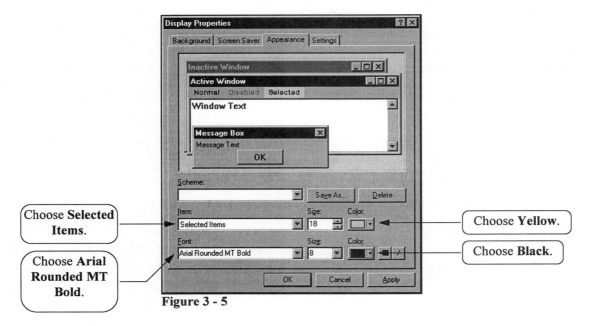

Figure 3 - 5

7. Open the **Item:** drop-down list box and click on **Selected Items**.

   *When **Selected Items** is chosen, the Font selections become active because selected items consist of text (Figure 3-5).*

8. At the **Color:** box to the right of the **Item:** box, choose **Yellow** for *Selected Items*.

9. At the **Font:** list, choose **Arial Rounded MT Bold**.

10. At the **Color:** box to the right of the **Font:** list, choose **Black** as the color for text.

11. Click on **OK**.

    Your selected changes have been applied to the Desktop.

12. At the Control Panel window, open the **File** menu.

    *You can see the effect of the selections you made. The font used for the menu items is Arial Rounded MT Bold. Also, items are highlighted in yellow (Figure 3-6). You will now select the **Desert** color scheme.*

The font is Arial Rounded MT Bold.

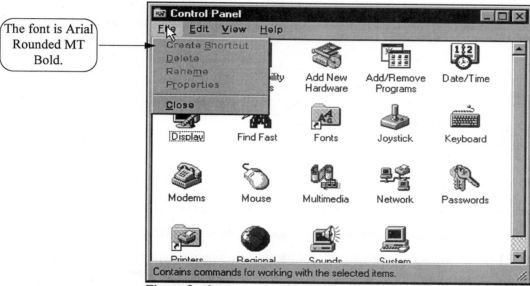

Figure 3 - 6

13. Close the **File** menu.

14. At the **Control Panel** window, double-click on the **Display** icon.

15. Click on the **Appearance** index tab.

16. Select **Desert** from the **Scheme** list box.

17. Click on **OK** to reset the color to **Desert** and notice it overrides not only the **Eggplant** color scheme, but also the custom changes that you made.

    The Control Panel window will still be maximized. Notice the new color scheme.

17. Leave the Control Panel open for the next activity.

Working with the Screen Saver

A screen saver is a moving pattern that will appear on your monitor after your computer has not been operated for a specified interval of time. Its purpose is to prevent the damage caused by the image "burning" into the glass of the monitor.

Windows 95 comes with five different screen savers. They are listed and described in Table 3-2. You may have additional or different screen savers, depending on how your computer has been set up.

Screen Saver	Description
Blank Screen	The Blank Screen saver shows only a black screen.
Flying Windows	Flying Windows icons move toward the user.
Marquee	You input the text that will move across the screen. The effect is similar to a theater marquee.
Mystify	A pattern of lines and triangles moves around the screen in a circular motion. The triangles change color as they move.
Starfield Simulation	Dots move toward the user in the same motion as the Flying Windows screen saver.

Table 3 - 2

There are three other options available to you when selecting a screen saver. You can change settings for the screen savers, for example, the number and speed of "Flying Windows." You can also preview the screen saver and set the interval after which the screen saver is displayed.

To select a screen saver:

- Click on the **Start** button on the Taskbar.

- Point to **Settings** and click on **Control Panel**.

- Double-click on the **Display** icon .

  The Display Properties window appears on the screen.

- Click on the **Screen Saver** index tab.

- Select a screen saver from the **Screen Saver** list box.

  The screen saver will be displayed in the sample computer at the top of the dialog box.

- Click on the **Settings** button to change the settings for the screen saver.

  NOTE: *The **Settings** dialog box will be different for each screen saver. Options that can be changed include the number of icons onscreen, the speed of the objects moving onscreen, text options, and background color.*

- Click on the **Preview** button to see the screen saver displayed.

- Select the amount of time allotted before the screen saver is activated.

- Click on **OK**.

Activity 3.4: Selecting a Screen Saver

In this activity you will select several of the screen savers available in *Windows 95* and edit the settings to change the way the screen saver appears on the screen.

1. After Activity 3.3, the Control Panel window should still be open and maximized. If it is not, select **SETTINGS/Control Panel** from the **Start** menu.

2. Double-click on the **Display** icon.

   The Display Properties window appears on the screen.

3. Click on the **Screen Saver** index tab.

*The **Screen Saver** tab appears in the Display Properties window (Figure 3-7). You will select the Flying Windows screen saver first.*

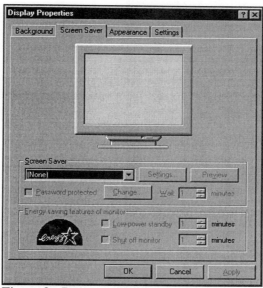

Figure 3 - 7

4. Write down the current screen saver so that you can change it back at the end of this activity.

5. Open the list under **Screen Saver** and click on **Flying Windows** from the **Screen Saver** list box (Figure 3-8).

Click on **Flying Windows** from the **Screen Saver** list box.

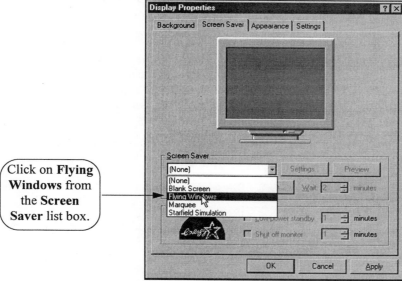

Figure 3 - 8

*The Flying Windows screen saver is demonstrated on the sample computer in the top portion of the dialog box (Figure 3-9). You can see a demonstration of the screen saver on the full screen by clicking on the **Preview** button.*

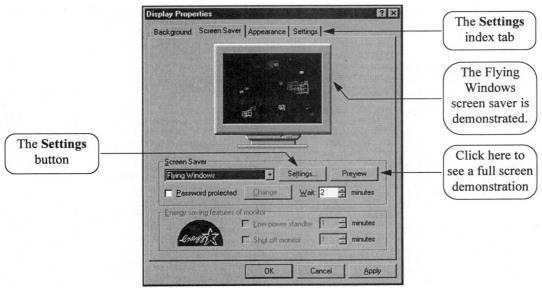

Figure 3 - 9

6. Click on the **Preview** button.

   A sample of the Flying Windows screen saver appears on the full screen.

7. Move the mouse slightly to stop the preview and return to the **Screen Saver** panel.

   Next you will select the Marquee screen saver, change the settings, and then preview the results.

8. Select **Marquee** from the **Screen Saver** list box.

   PROBLEM SOLVER: *Depending on how your computer has been set up, you may have the **Marquee** selection or one that is slightly different. Another possible name for this screen saver is **Scrolling Marquee**. If neither of these screen saver names appears in the **Screen Saver** list box, ask your instructor or lab assistant which screen saver to select.*

9. Click on the **Settings** *button* next to **Marquee,** (**not** the **Settings** index tab).

   *The **Marquee Setup** dialog box appears on the screen (Figure 3-10). The Marquee screen saver is a useful way to leave a message on your computer while you are not there. Screen savers also are a convenient method of concealing your work while you step away from your desk. You will change the text of the Marquee screen saver, format the text, and then change the background color.*

10. Click at the beginning of the **Text** box so that the cursor appears in front of the first character (see Figure 3-10).

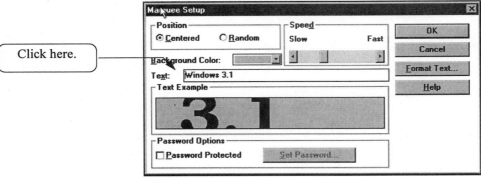

Figure 3 - 10

11. Highlight the current text by holding the left mouse button down and dragging the cursor over the text (Figure 3-11).

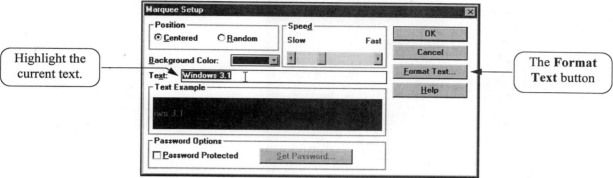

Highlight the current text.

The **Format Text** button

Figure 3 - 11

12. Type the following line of text.

   Stepped away...will be back shortly.

   Since the current text is highlighted, the new text you type in will automatically replace it.

13. Click on the **Format Text** button (see Figure 3-11).

   *The **Format Text** dialog box appears on-screen (Figure 3-12). You will change the font (typeface), color, and size of the text. Use Figure 3-12 to locate the parts of the **Format Text** dialog box referenced in steps 14–16.*

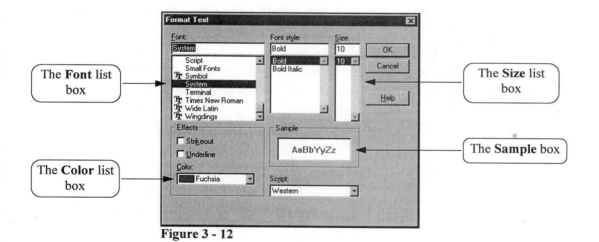

The **Font** list box

The **Size** list box

The **Sample** box

The **Color** list box

Figure 3 - 12

14. Scroll up on the **Font** list box and click on **Bookman Old Style**.

    PROBLEM SOLVER: *If the Bookman Old Style font is not available, select another True Type font. True Type fonts have a **TT** icon* **T͞T** *to the left of the font name.*

   A sample of the text appears in the Sample box.

15. Scroll down on the **Size** list box and click on **72**.

   Size refers to the Point Size, or printed height of the characters. There are about 72 points in one inch; thus you have chosen a printed height (not screen height) of approximately 1" for the characters in your message.

16. Select any color from the **Color** drop-down list box at the bottom left of the box. Your screen should resemble Figure 3-13.

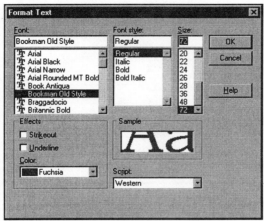

Figure 3 - 13

17. Click on **OK**.

    *You will return to the **Marquee Setup** dialog box. The final step to changing the setup is selecting a color for the background of the screen.*

18. Select a color for the background which is compatible with the text color you selected from the **Background Color** drop-down list box.

19. Click on **OK**.

    *You will return to the **Screen Saver** tab. Now you will preview the screen saver on the full screen.*

20. Click on the **Preview** button.

    A sample of the Marquee screen saver appears on the full screen (Figure 3-14).

    Be careful not to move the mouse too soon or the preview will disappear.

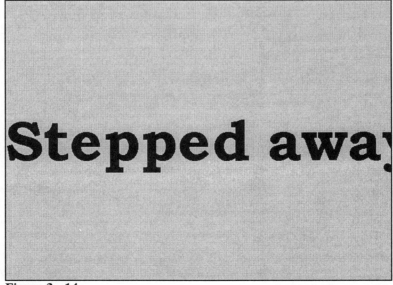

Figure 3 - 14

21. Move the mouse to stop the screen saver and return to the **Screen Saver** tab.

    You will change the wait time of the screen saver. The wait time is the amount of time the computer allows without activity before the screen saver begins. The wait time option is a spin box. To change the number in a spin box, click on the ⬆ or the ⬇ to increase or decrease the number.

22. Click on the ⬇ in the **Wait** spin box until **1 minute** has been selected.

23. Click on **OK**.

    You will return to the Control Panel window. Now you will view the screen saver as it operates according to the settings you just selected.

24. Do not move the mouse or type for 1 minute.

    The Marquee screen saver will appear on-screen.

25. Move the mouse to return to the Desktop and the Control Panel window.

26. To return to the Display Properties window so that you can change back to the original settings, double-click on the **Display** icon.

27. Click on the **Background** index tab and change the Pattern and Wallpaper settings back to the selections recorded earlier.

28. Click on the **Appearance** tab and change the color scheme back to the one you recorded earlier.

29. Click on the **Screen Saver** tab and change the screen saver back to the original selection.

30. Click on **OK** to return to the Control Panel window.

31. Leave the Control Panel open for the next activity.

CHANGING THE MOUSE OPTIONS

The mouse options will help you customize the way the mouse operates. You might think about changing mouse options if you are left-handed, if you have trouble double-clicking, if you find the mouse pointer too small, if the pointer moves too fast, or if you sometimes lose track of the mouse pointer. The two options you will explore here are changing the mouse for left-handed users and changing the speed of double-clicking.

To change the mouse configuration to left-handed:

- Click on the **Start** button.

- Point to **SETTINGS** and click on **Control Panel**.

- Double-click on the **Mouse** icon.
  *The **Mouse Properties** dialog box appears on-screen.*

- Click on the **Buttons** index tab.

- Click on the **Left-handed** button.

- Click on **Apply**.

- Test the mouse by double-clicking the right mouse button on the Jack-in-the-Box in the Test area.

- Click on **OK**.

To change the double-click speed:

- Click on the **Start** button.
- Point to **Settings** and click on **Control Panel**.
- Double-click on the **Mouse** icon.

    *The **Mouse Properties** dialog box appears on the screen.*

- Click on the **Buttons** tab, if it is not showing.
- Point to the slide tab on the **Double-click speed** ruler and drag it to the desired speed.
- Test the double-click speed in the **Test** area by double-clicking on the Jack-in-the-Box.
- Click on **OK**.

Activity 3.5: Changing Mouse Options

In this activity you will change the mouse to a left-handed configuration and slow down the double-click speed of the mouse.

1. After Activity 3.4, the Control Panel window should still be open and maximized. If it is not, select **SETTINGS/Control Panel** from the **Start** menu.

2. Double-click on the **Mouse** icon.

    *The **Mouse Properties** dialog box appears on the screen (Figure 3-15).*

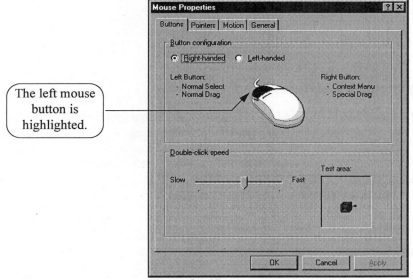

The left mouse button is highlighted.

Figure 3 - 15

3. Click on the **Buttons** index tab.

    *The **Buttons** panel appears with options for Button configuration and Double-click speed. Look at the sample mouse below the radio buttons in the Button configuration area. The left button is highlighted and the operations for the left button are listed as **Normal Select** and **Normal Drag** (see Figure 3-15).*

4. Click on the **Left-handed** button.

    *Look at the picture of the mouse below the buttons. The right button is highlighted and the operations for the right button are now listed as **Normal Select** and **Normal Drag** (Figure 3-16). Therefore, the operation of the buttons has been reversed.*

Button configuration options

Double-click speed options

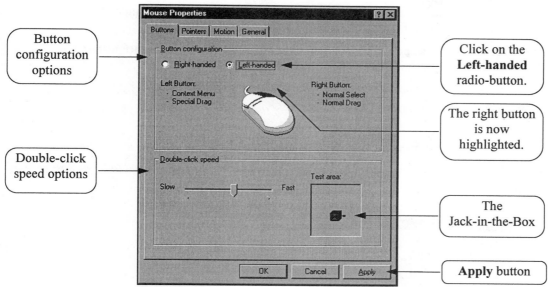

Click on the **Left-handed** radio-button.

The right button is now highlighted.

The Jack-in-the-Box

Apply button

Figure 3 - 16

5. Click on the **Apply** button (see Figure 3-16).

6. Test the mouse by double-clicking the right mouse button on the Jack-in-the-Box in the Test area.

   Jack will jump out of the box! This would happen if you double-clicked the left mouse button in the right-handed mouse configuration.

7. Click the left mouse button on **Jack**.

   *A **What's This?** pop-up appears. It is a Help feature, giving you a definition of the feature you clicked on.*

8. Highlight **What's This?** and click the right mouse button (Figure 3-17).

   The definition describing the test area appears.

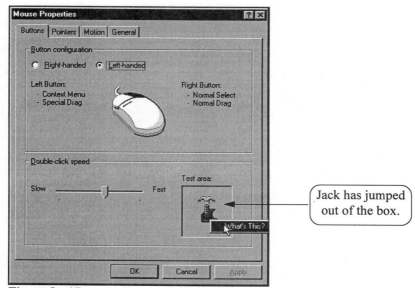

Jack has jumped out of the box.

Figure 3 - 17

9. Click the right mouse button once to remove the definition, and then double-click the right mouse button to return Jack to the box.

10. **Return the button configuration to right-handed by clicking on the Right-handed button. Remember to click the right button of the mouse.**

11. Click on **Apply**. Again, use the right button.

    Now you will change the double-click speed of the mouse. From now on you may use the left button.

12. Point to the slide tab on the **Double-click speed** ruler and drag it all the way to the left.

    Dragging the tab all the way to the left slows down the double-click speed to its slowest speed (Figure 3-18).

The slide tab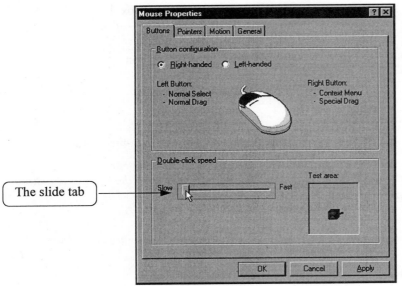

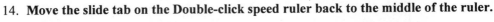

Figure 3 - 18

13. Test the double-click speed out by double-clicking on **Jack-in-the-Box**.

    Make sure you wait a second before executing the second click. Jack will jump out of the box.

14. **Move the slide tab on the Double-click speed ruler back to the middle of the ruler.**

 PROBLEM SOLVER: *It is important that you leave the double-click setting in the middle of the ruler. If the speed is too fast or slow, the next user may be unable to use the mouse.*

15. Test the speed by double-clicking on the Jack-in-the-Box.

    This will return Jack to the box.

16. Click on **OK**.

    You will return to the Desktop and the Control Panel window.

16. Leave the Control Panel open for the next activity.

CHANGING THE DATE AND TIME

Not all computers keep perfect time. If you notice that the time showing on the Taskbar is incorrect, you can change it using the Date/Time option in the Control Panel. A useful option in the Date/Time section is the option to have the computer account for the changing of daylight saving time. Another useful option is the Time Zone option. The Time Zone option allows users to keep track of files or messages that have been sent. This is a great feature for users who are involved in international business or involved with the Internet, because they need to know what time it is in various time zones.

To change the date and time:

- Click on the **Start** button.
- Point to **SETTINGS** and click on **Control Panel**.
- Double-click on the **Date/Time** icon.

  *The **Date/Time Properties** dialog box appears on the screen.*

- Click on the **Date & Time** index tab.
- Select the desired month and year from the list boxes located above the calendar in the Date area.
- Click on the desired day in the calendar.
- Double-click on the desired option you would like to change in the time (hour, minutes, seconds, am/pm).

  You need to click only once on the am/pm option.

- Click on the ⬆ or ⬇ to increase or decrease the numbers. The am/pm option will toggle back and forth between the two options.
- Click on **OK**.

To select the automatic Day Light Saving option:

- Click on the **Start** button.
- Point to **SETTINGS** and click on **Control Panel**.
- Double-click on the **Date/Time** icon.

  *The **Date/Time Properties** dialog box appears on the screen.*

- Click on the **Time Zone** index tab.
- If a check does not appear in the check box labeled, *Automatically adjust clock for daylight saving changes*, click on the check box.
- Click on **OK**.

Activity 3.6: Using the Date/Time Options

In this activity you will change the date and time for your computer, and then select the automatic option for daylight saving changes, if it is not already selected.

1. After Activity 3.5, the Control Panel window should still be open and maximized. If it is not, select **SETTINGS/Control Panel** from the **Start** menu.

Date/Time

2. Double-click on the **Date/Time** icon.

   *The **Date/Time Properties** dialog box appears on-screen (Figure 3-19).*

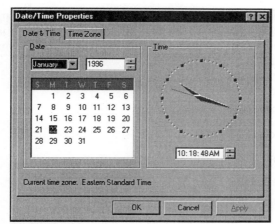

Figure 3 - 19

3. Click on the **Date & Time** index tab.

   You will change the date to your birthday, keeping the current year.

4. Select your *birth month* from the drop-down list in the Date section.

5. Click on your *birth day* in the Calendar area of the Date section.

   Next, you will change the current time. Often the clock in a computer can speed up or slow down. Let's assume that the time on your computer is 10 minutes fast. You will change the minutes section.

6. Double-click on the minutes section of the time showing below the clock in the Time section.

   The minutes section is highlighted (Figure 3-20).

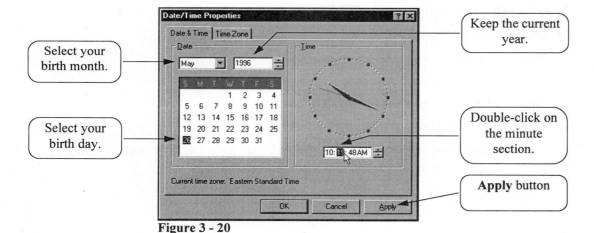

Figure 3 - 20

7. Click on the ↓ spinner next to the time until the minutes are 10 minutes before the current time.

8. Click on the **Apply** button.

   The new date and time will be applied to your computer.

9. Check this out by pointing to the date on the far right of the Taskbar until the currently set date appears.

The date and time should match your changes. Notice that the day of the week also appears with the date. The date will disappear after a few seconds.

10. Change the date back to the current date using the method described in Steps 4 and 5.

11. Change the time back to the current time using the method described in Steps 6 and 7.

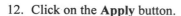

    HINT: *You will use the ↑ spinner to increase the time.*

12. Click on the **Apply** button.

    Now you will turn on the automatic daylight saving changes option, if it is not already on. This option will automatically account for daylight saving time without you having to change the time.

13. Click on the **Time Zone** index tab.

    *The **Time Zone** tab appears on the screen (Figure 3-21). The current time zone is listed with a picture of the current time zone below the list box. The **Automatically adjust clock for daylight saving changes** check box is below the map.*

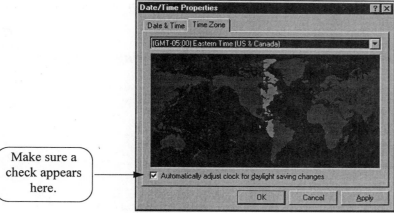

Make sure a check appears here. ———→

Figure 3 - 21

14. If there is no check in the box, click in the check box.

15. Click on **OK**.

    You will return to the Desktop and the Control Panel window.

16. Close the Control Panel window.

SUMMARY

In this lesson you learned about the Control Panel and the options that are available to make *Windows 95* "look and feel" the way you want it to. The Control Panel lets you set and keep your own preferences for *Windows 95*. Appearance options change the look of the Desktop. To change the appearance of the Desktop, you changed the background by selecting both a pattern and wallpaper, selected a color scheme for all the components of the Desktop, and selected a screen saver. Working with a mouse can often be tricky, especially if you are a first time mouse user or you are left-handed. You changed the mouse setting to left-handed mouse and also changed the double-click speed. Finally, because not all computers keep perfect time, the date and time was changed using the Date/Time option.

KEY TERMS

Accessibility Options	Fonts	Passwords
Add New Hardware	Keyboard	Pattern
Add/Remove Programs	Left-handed Mouse	Printers
Background	Mail and Fax	Regional Settings
Color Scheme	Microsoft Mail Postoffice	Screen Saver
Control Panel	Modems	Sounds
Date/Time	Mouse	System
Day Light Savings Option	Multimedia	Wallpaper
Desktop	Network	
Display	ODBC	

INDEPENDENT PROJECTS

The four independent projects will allow you to practice changing the settings options in the Control Panel. Independent Projects 3.1, 3.2, and 3.3 reinforce topics that have been covered in this lesson. Independent Project 3.4 challenges you to use the Font option, available at the Control Panel, to look at the fonts accessible on your computer, and create printouts of some of these fonts.

Independent Project 3.1: Customizing your Desktop by Selecting a Pattern and a Color Scheme

In this project you will change the pattern and color scheme of your Desktop.

1. Open the Control Panel window.

2. Double-click on the **Display** button.

3. Click on the **Background** tab.

4. Write down the current Wallpaper and Pattern selections.

5. Choose **(None)** in the **Wallpaper** drop-down list box.

6. Select a pattern you like from the **Pattern** drop-down list box.

7. Click on the **Appearance** tab.

8. Write down the current color scheme.

9. Choose a color scheme from the **Scheme** drop-down list box.

10. Click on **OK**.

11. Minimize the Control Panel window so you can see the effect of your selections.

    How does the pattern look with the color scheme you selected?

11. Click the Control Panel button on the Taskbar to return the window to its previous size.

12. Change the settings for the Wallpaper, Pattern, and Color Scheme back to what they were before you made changes.

13. Close the Control Panel window.

Independent Project 3.2: Customizing your Desktop by Selecting Wallpaper and a Screen Saver

In this project you will customize your Desktop by selecting wallpaper for the background and a screen saver.

1. Open the Control Panel window.

2. Double-click on the **Display** button.

3. Click on the **Background** tab.

4. Write down the current selections for **Pattern** and **Wallpaper**, so that you can return to the original settings after this project.

5. Choose **(None)** in the **Pattern** drop-down list box.

6. Select a wallpaper selection that you like from the **Wallpaper** drop-down list box.

7. Click on the **Tile** radio button.

8. Click on the **Screen Saver** tab.

9. Write down the currently selected screen saver so that you can return to this screen saver after this project.

10. Select the **Marquee** screen saver from the **Screen Saver** list box.

    PROBLEM SOLVER: *Depending on how your computer has been set up, you may have the **Marquee** selection or one that is slightly different. Another possible name for this screen saver is **Scrolling Marquee**. If neither of these screen saver names appears in the **Screen Saver** list box, ask your instructor or lab assistant which screen saver to select.*

11. Click on the **Settings** button.

12. Type in the text for the screen saver in the **Text** box.

13. Select a background color.

14. Click on the **Format Text** button.

15. Select a font, font style, and size for the text of your screen saver.

16. Select the color for the text, and then click on **OK**.

17. Click on **OK** again to return to the **Screen Saver** tab.

18. Click on the **Preview** button to see the screen saver displayed on the full screen, and then move the mouse so that you return to the **Screen Saver** tab.

19. Select **1 minute** from the **Wait** spin box.

20. Click on **OK**.

21. Wait 1 minute without touching the keyboard or the mouse so that the screen saver appears on the screen.

22. Move the mouse to remove the screen saver from the screen.

23. Change the settings for the Wallpaper, Pattern, and Screen Saver back to what they were before you made changes.

24. Close the Control Panel window.

Independent Project 3.3: Customizing the Mouse and the Date/Time Options on your Computer

In this project you will customize the mouse and the date/time options. You will change the double-click speed of the mouse, and then you will change the date and time on your computer.

1. Open the Control Panel window.

2. Double-click on the **Mouse** icon.

    *The **Mouse Properties** dialog box appears on the screen.*

3. Click on the **Buttons** index tab.

4. Point to the slide tab on the **Double-click speed** ruler and drag it all the way to the right.

5. Try double-clicking the Jack-in-the-Box in the Test area.

   Can you do it?

6. Change the double-click speed to the slowest speed.

7. Now double-click on the Jack-in-the Box in the Test area. Try double-clicking several times at different speeds.

   Does double-clicking work each time? How does slowing down the speed affect the mouse?

8. **Change the double-click speed to medium, half-way between Slow and Fast.**

9. Return to the Control Panel window.

10. Double-click on the **Date/Time** icon.

    *The **Date/Time Properties** dialog box appears on the screen.*

11. Click on the **Date & Time** tab, if it is not showing.

12. Select the month in which you plan to take your next vacation from the list box.

13. Click on the approximate day your vacation will begin on the calendar.

14. Keep the current year showing in the spin box.

15. Click on the time that is showing on the right side of the Taskbar.

    What appears above the current time?

16. Change the month and day back to the current date. **Don't forget to do this!**

17. Click on **OK** to close the Date/Time Properties window, and then close the Control Panel window.

Independent Project 3.4: Using the Fonts Option in the Control Panel

In this project you will use the Fonts option in the Control Panel window to look at several of the fonts that are available on your computer, and then you will print out an information sheet about the font. This information sheet lists the font name, its file size, the current version number, as well as how the font looks at different sizes.

   This could be helpful if you were deciding on fonts to use in a project. You could print out several of your choices and look at them side by side. What other possible uses can you think of?

   This project is a challenge exercise. This material has not been covered in the lesson.

1. Open the Control Panel window.

Fonts

2. Double-click on the **Fonts** icon.

   The Fonts window appears on the screen.

3. Click on **VIEW/Large Icons**.

   Your screen should resemble Figure 3-22. The contents of the Fonts window will not match exactly because you will have different fonts on your computer.

4. Double-click on one of the font icons.

   The window for the font you selected appears on the screen.

5. Maximize the window for the font you selected.

   Your window will resemble Figure 3-23. It will not match exactly because of the font you selected.

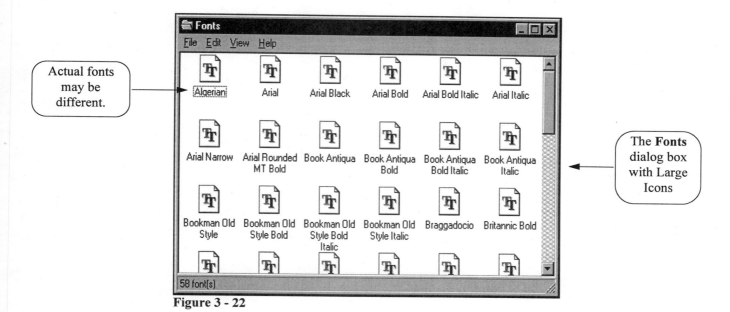

Actual fonts may be different.

The Fonts dialog box with Large Icons

Figure 3 - 22

The Print button

Figure 3 - 23

6. Click on the **Print** button, which is located under the **Minimize**, **Maximize**, and **Close** buttons.

7. Click on **OK** when the **Print** dialog box appears to create a printout for the font.

8. To return to the Fonts window, click on the **Done** button located under the Title bar.

9. Select another font from the Fonts window.

10. Print out the font information.

11. Return to the Fonts window.

12. Close the Fonts window.

13. Close the Control Panel window.

4 Using Help

Objectives

In this lesson you will learn how to:

- Understand Help options that are available in *Windows 95*
- Access Help
- Use the Help Contents index tab

- Use the Help Index tab
- Use the Help Find index tab
- Print a Help topic

HELP OPTIONS IN WINDOWS 95

In the *Windows 95* environment, there are a number of ways in which to find answers to the questions you will inevitably have.

First, every program you run will display Help as the last item on its Menu Bar. Second, many dialog boxes contain a small Help button next to the Close button. Third, in *Windows 95*, Help also appears on the **Start** menu.

Although you reach Help directly from your application program, Help is actually a separate program that opens and runs in its own window. Therefore, if you have opened Help while working in a program, you may find that it is still running when you have closed the program.

Help is organized in three panels reached by index tabs: **Contents**, **Index**, and **Find.** Click on the **Contents** index tab to find topics grouped by subject, the **Index** tab to find topics that are listed alphabetically, or the **Find** tab to find all the topics that contain a specific word or phrase. We will explore these three kinds of Help in this lesson.

HOW TO ACCESS HELP

The most direct method for getting Help is to click on the **Start** button and then click on Help. Two shortcut methods are also available. If a dialog box is open and it has a **Help** button in the top right corner, you can click on the Help button and then click on the item you need help with. You can also point and click the *right mouse button* on the part of the dialog box you want help for, and then select **What's This?** from the menu that appears.

REMEMBER: *Read the bulleted list that follows, but do not actually perform the steps until you reach Activity 4.1.*

To open the Help dialog box:

- Click on the **Start** button.
- Click on **Help**.

    *The **Help Topics: Windows Help** dialog box will appear.*

- Click on the index tab that seems appropriate.

To use the Help button to access Help:

- From a dialog box that has a **Help** button  in the top right corner next to the **Close** button, click on the **Help** button.

  The mouse pointer will have a question mark attached to it.

- Click on the item you need help with.

  Help will appear in its own window for the item you selected.

To use the right mouse button to access Help:

- Point to the item you need help with.
- Click the right mouse button.

  A pop-up menu will appear.

- Select **What's This?**

  A definition or explanation of the selected item will appear.

Activity 4.1: Accessing Help

In this activity, you will access Help in three ways: using the **Help** button, using the right mouse button, and using the Help command on the **Start** menu.

1. Turn on your computer, if it is not already on.

    *You will open the Control Panel window and use the **Help** button and right mouse button methods of accessing Help.*

2. Click on the **Start** menu.

3. Point to **SETTINGS**, and then click on **Control Panel**.

    *The Control Panel window appears. The **Help** button is not available in this window, but you can get Help at the Menu Bar (see Figure 4-1).*

Figure 4 - 1

Date/Time

4. To Open the **Date/Time** application, double-click on the **Date/Time** icon.

    *This window has a **Help** button in the top right corner of the window (Figure 4-2). You will use the **Help** button to get Help for the Calendar.*

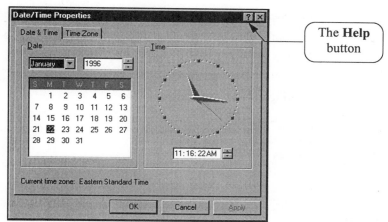

The **Help** button

Figure 4 - 2

5. Click on the **Date & Time** index tab.

6. Click on the **Help** button located to the left of the **Close** button.

    The mouse pointer will have a question mark attached to it.

7. Point anywhere on the calendar and click the left mouse button.

    A pop-up box appears with the help information about the calendar (Figure 4-3).

> Displays the days that correspond to the selected month and year settings. The highlighted date is the one your computer is currently using.

Figure 4 - 3

8. After reading the Help information, click the mouse again or press **ESC** to remove the box.

    Now you will use the right mouse button to access Help. You will get Help for the clock.

9. Point to the clock, and then click the right mouse button.

    *A small menu saying **What's This?** appears (Figure 4-4).*

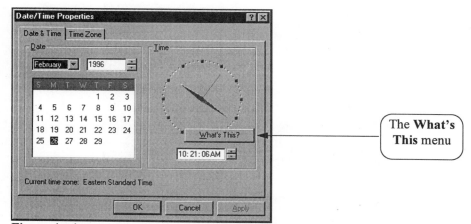

The **What's This** menu

Figure 4 - 4

10. Click on **What's This?**

    A similar pop-up box with Help information appears.

11. After reading the information, click again to remove the box.

    *Now you will close the open windows, then use the **Start** menu to access Help.*

12. Click on the **Close** buttons for the Date/Time Properties window and the Control Panel window.

13. Click on the **Start** menu.

14. Click on **Help** (see Figure 4-5).

Figure 4 - 5

*The **Help Topics: Windows Help** window appears (Figure 4-6). This is the same feature that is available from the Menu Bar of the Control Panel window. Notice the **Contents**, **Index**, and **Find** index tabs. These Help features will be discussed in the next three sections.*

The **Contents, Index**, and **Find** index tabs →

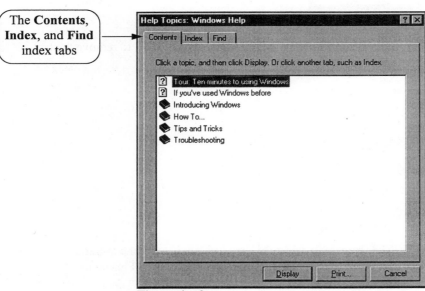

Figure 4 - 6

15. Click on the **Contents** index tab.

16. Leave **Help** open for the next activity.

THE CONTENTS TAB

The **Contents** tab of the Help window organizes Help information hierarchically by subject. The information is arranged in a dynamic outline similar to a table of contents. You will be able to collapse or expand the levels of the contents list by clicking the mouse.

The icons associated with the **Contents** tab are the closed book ![closed book icon] , the open book ![open book icon] , and the Help document ![help document icon] . The closed book represents the top level of a subject. Double-clicking on either the book or text will expand the list. When expanded, the closed book icon will change to an open book with other subject headings below. When you see a Help document icon, you will be able to double-click to open the Help document and read the Help material.

When the **Contents** panel is first viewed, it contains a list of closed book icons and Help document icons. The number will vary depending on how *Windows 95* was installed on your computer. One of the available Help documents answers questions commonly asked by users of previous versions of *Windows*.

To open a Help topic:

- In the **Help Topics: Windows Help** window, click on the **Contents** tab.
- Double-click on the **top level subject heading** you desire or click on a topic, and then click on the **Open** button at the bottom of the dialog box.
- Continue double-clicking on subject headings (books) until you see the Help topic (document) that interests you.
- Double-click on the Help topic or click on the Help topic, and then click on the **Display** button.

  Notice the difference in command buttons. If you are opening a book, the command button is **Open** *and if you are opening or displaying a Help topic, the command button is* **Display**. *When you double-click on a Help topic or click on a Help topic and then click on* **Display**, *the Help topic will be displayed in a window.*

  If a bulleted list with gray buttons is displayed, you will be able to click on a button to display a topic. If the topic you want help for concerns a window, you can go to the window by clicking on the gray button with an arrow.

- After reading the Help topic, close the Help topic by clicking on its **Close** button.

  NOTE: *Depending on the topic that you selected, you may return to the Desktop or you may return to the Help Topics: Windows Help window. If you return to the Help Topics: Windows Help window, close that window also.*

To get answers to frequently asked questions if you have used a previous version of Windows:

- In the **Help Topics: Windows Help** window, click on the **Contents** index tab.
- Double-click on the Help topic, **If you've used Windows before,** or click on the topic, and then click on the **Display** button.

  The Windows Help window appears with topics listed as bullets on the left side of the window and an area to demonstrate answers to commonly asked questions.

- Click on the square gray bullet before a question.

  The answer to the question will be displayed on the right side of the window with an illustration shown below the answer.

- Continue clicking on questions for which you want to see answers.
- Close the Windows Help window by clicking on its **Close** button.

Activity 4.2: Using the Contents Tab

In this activity you will use the **Contents** tab to find Help. You will use Help that is designed to answer frequently asked questions about *Windows 95.*

1. After Activity 4.1, you should have the Help Topics: Windows Help window showing on the screen. If not, click on the **Start** button, and then click on **Help.**

2. Click on the **Contents** index tab.

    The **Contents** *tab appears in the Help Topics: Windows Help window (Figure 4-7).*

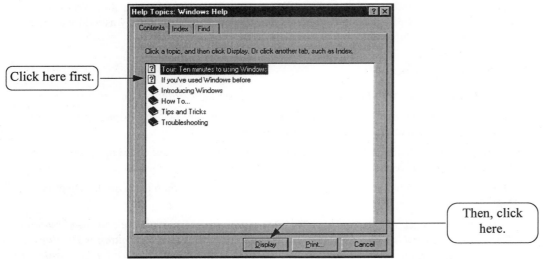

Figure 4 - 7

3. Click on the Help Topic, **If you've used Windows before**, and then click on the **Display** button.

    The Windows Help window appears (Figure 4-8).

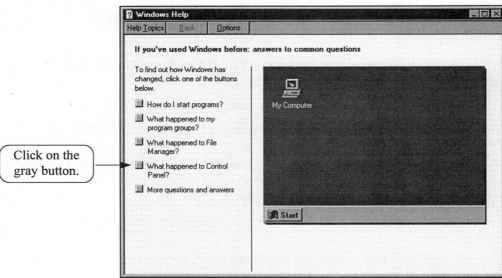

Figure 4 - 8

4. Click on the gray square button before the topic, **What happened to Control Panel?**

   The answer to the question is displayed on the right side of the window with an illustration of the answer below it (Figure 4-9).

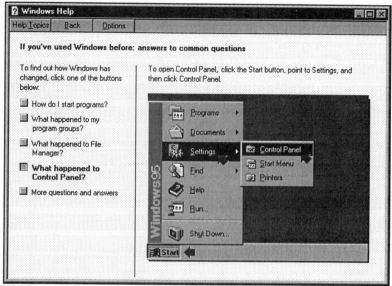

Figure 4 - 9

5. Now click on the bullet for **More questions and answers**.

   Another list of questions appears.

6. Click on the bullet for **Where did the MS-DOS prompt go?**

   *Again, the answer and its illustration appear on the right side of the window. Now you will return to the **Contents** tab.*

7. Click on the **Help Topics** button below the Title bar (Figure 4-10).

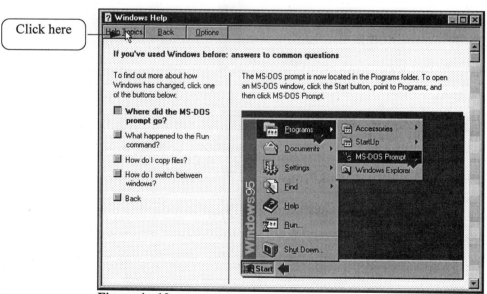

Figure 4 - 10

*There are four **top level subject headings** displayed. Each has a book icon showing, signifying that there is information below. The four subject headings are: **Introducing Windows, How To..., Tips and Tricks,** and **Troubleshooting**. Depending on which heading you select, you may find more subject headings (books) or **Help topics** (documents).*

8. Click on the Help subject, **Introducing Windows**, and then click on the **Open** button.

*Several more Help subjects appear one level below **Introducing Windows: Welcome** and **Using Windows Accessories.** Notice that the closed book icon changes to an open book.*

PROBLEM SOLVER: *The number of topics will vary depending on how Windows 95 has been installed on your computer. Windows 95 can be installed on your computer using a 3½'' disk version or a CD-ROM version. The CD-ROM version has additional files. During the installation process, you can also choose not to have certain files installed on your computer. In either case, this causes minor differences when Help windows are displayed on the screen. Be aware that the number of Help topics on your screen may not match exactly.*

9. Open the **Using Windows Accessories** book by double-clicking on the closed book icon.

*The Help Contents list continues to expand with six more topics listed below **Using Windows Accessories**.*

10. Open the **For Writing and Drawing** book by double-clicking on its book icon.

*Three Help topics are listed below **For Writing and Drawing** (Figure 4-11).*

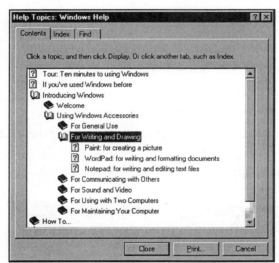

Figure 4 - 11

11. Click on the **WordPad: for writing and formatting documents** Help topic, and then click on the **Display** button.

*Windows Help for **Using WordPad to write and format documents** appears (Figure 4-12). Two interactive **Help** buttons appear in this Help window. By clicking on the gray square button you will see a list of related topics. To start WordPad, you can click on the gray square button with the curved arrow.*

12. Click on the arrow button to start *WordPad*.

WordPad is opened and the Help window is placed in front of the WordPad window so that you can read the Help topic and see the WordPad program. However, there is minimal information on WordPad in Windows Help. You can get complete WordPad Help by clicking on the Help command on the WordPad Menu Bar (Figure 4-13).

13. Click on the **Related Topics** button.

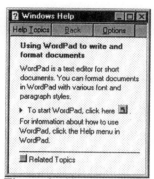

Figure 4 - 12

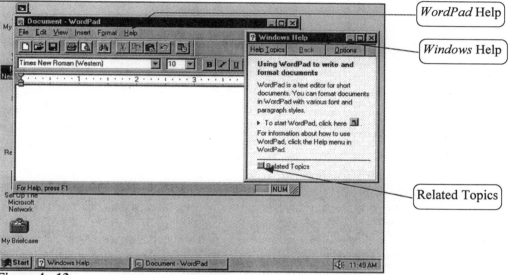

Figure 4 - 13

A Topics Found window appears above the Windows Help window (Figure 4-14). In this instance, only one related topic was found: **Accessories: Using Notepad to write and edit text files**.

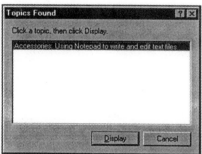

Figure 4 - 14

14. Click on the **Display** button.

*A Windows Help window similar to the one for WordPad appears (Figure 4-15). Notice the same two buttons appear: the square gray button for **Related Topics** and the square gray button with an arrow to start Notepad.*

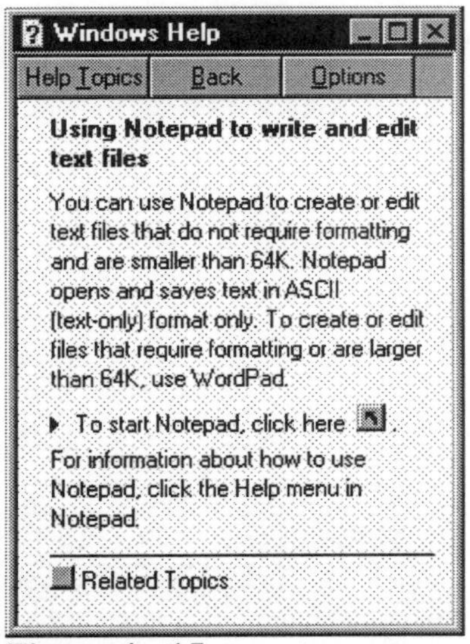

Figure 4 - 15

PROBLEM SOLVER: *You may need to use the scroll bars to see the rest of the Windows Help topic. The size of the Help window that appears on the screen may vary. Scroll bars will automatically appear in a window in which all the available information is not displayed.*

15. Close the Windows Help window.
16. Close *WordPad.*

    You will return to the Desktop.

THE INDEX TAB

The **Index** panel organizes Help topics alphabetically. You can type the first few letters of the topic and then look for the topic on the list. Using the **Index** panel, you can see all of the subtopics for a given topic at one time. This is useful if you know the general but not specific name of the topic for which you want help. For example, if you want help about opening and closing programs using the Taskbar, but you are not sure how this subtopic would be worded, you might try **open, close**, and finally **Taskbar** until you find the subtopic you want.

To access Help using the Index tab:

- In the **Help Topics: Windows Help** window, click on the **Index** tab.

  *The **Index** tab appears in the Help Topics: Windows Help window.*
- Type the first few letters of the topic you want help with.

  The index list will change as you enter in each letter.
- On the list of entries, click on the topic or subtopic.
- Click on the **Display** button.

  The Help window will appear.
- After reading and/or printing the Help information, close the Help window.

NOTE: *Depending on the Help topic that you selected, you may return to the Desktop or you may return to the Help Topics: Windows Help window. If you return to the Help Topics: Windows Help window, close that window also.*

Activity 4.3: Using the Index Tab

In this activity you will use the **Index** tab to obtain Help about using the Taskbar.

1.   After Activity 4.2, all windows should be closed.

2.   Click on the **Start** button.

3.   Click on **Help**.

The Help Topics: Windows Help screen appears.

4.   Click on the **Index** tab, if it is not already showing.

*The **Index** tab appears in the Help Topics window (Figure 4-16).*

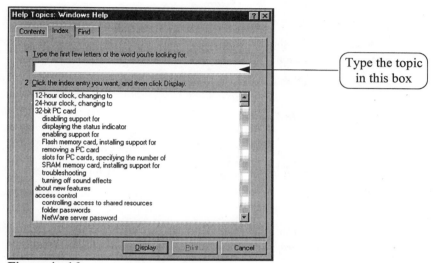

Figure 4 - 16

5.   Type **Taskbar** in the text box at the top of the dialog box. The box already contains the blinking cursor (Figure 4-16).

*The **Taskbar** heading will be selected in the index list below the text box. There are several subtopics under the main listing (Figure 4-17).*

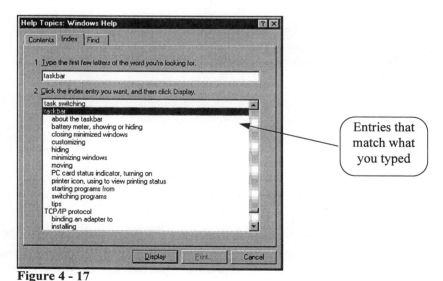

Figure 4 - 17

6. Click on the subtopic, **closing minimized windows**, and then click on the **Display** button.

   *A Windows Help window appears with Help for **closing a minimized window**. In the window, **Taskbar** appears in dotted and underlined green characters. Clicking on the term will display a definition.*

7. To get a definition of the term **taskbar**, click on the underlined item.

   *A definition of **taskbar** appears (Figure 4-18).*

The taskbar is the bar on your desktop that has the Start button on it. Buttons representing running programs appear on this bar.

Figure 4 - 18

8. Press **ESC** or click the left mouse button in a blank area of the Windows Help window to remove the definition.

   PROBLEM SOLVER: *If you click the left mouse button on the Desktop instead of on a blank area of the Windows Help window, you will close the window. If this happens, you will need to access Help again using the **Start** menu. You can return to the **Index** tab by clicking on the **Help Topics** button below the Title bar.*

9. To return to the **Index** tab, click on the **Help Topics** button.

   *You return to the Help Topics window with the **Index** tab showing.*

10. Click on the **Taskbar** subtopic, **starting programs from**, and then click on the **Display** button.

    *A Topics Found window appears with two subtopics (Figure 4-19). You will select the first topic, **Starting a program**.*

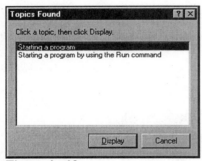

Figure 4 - 19

11. Click on **Starting a program**, if it is not already selected, and then click on the **Display** button in the Topics Found window.

    The Windows Help window appears with Help for starting programs. The first Tip listed explains how to start a program using the Taskbar.

12. To return to the Index tab, click on the **Help Topics** button.

    *You return to the **Index** tab. Notice that Help for starting programs also has some information for switching between programs.*

13. Click on the subtopic, **switching programs**, and then click on the **Display** button.

    *A Windows Help window is displayed with help for switching between programs. You are now finished using the **Index** tab to obtain help for the Taskbar. You will close the Windows Help window.*

14. To return to the Desktop, click on the **Close** button for the Windows Help window.

THE FIND TAB

The **Find** tab is useful when you know a word or a phrase you need help with. The **Find** tab finds all the topics that contain the word or phrase you type in.

There are several options that are available for the **Find** tab. You can search the Help database based on all the words you typed in any order, or on at least one of the words you typed. Or, you can display Help entries that begin with the characters you type, contain the characters you type, end with the characters you type, or match the characters you type. Finally, you can narrow the search by selecting only a few of the Help files.

To obtain Help using the Find tab:

- In the **Help Topics: Windows Help** window, click on the **Find** index tab.

  *The **Find** tab appears in the Help Topics window.*

- Type the word or phrase for which you want to obtain Help in the text box labeled: **Type the word(s) you want to find.**

  *A list of matching words that may narrow your search will appear in the list box labeled, **Select some matching words to narrow your search**.*

- If necessary, click on one of the matching words.

  A list of topics appears in the bottom list box. When you select a matching word, the number of topics in the topics list will decrease.

- Click on the desired topic.

- Click on the **Display** button.

To change the Find options:

- In the Help Topics: Windows Help window, click on the **Find** tab.

- Click on the **Options** button.

  The Find Options window appears. Options are available for how the search is conducted, characteristics of the words that are found, and how to begin searching.

- Select the desired options.

- Click on **OK**.

Activity 4.4: Using the Find Tab

In this activity you will use the **Find** tab to obtain Help in managing your files. Let's assume you have used the *Windows 3.1* File Manager and have just realized that it no longer exists in *Windows 95*. What has replaced it? You can use the **Find** tab to find what you are looking for.

1. After Activity 4.3, all windows should be closed.

2. Click on the **Start** button.

3. Click on **Help**.

    The Help Topics: Windows Help screen appears.

4. Click on the **Find** index tab.

    *The **Find** tab appears in the Help Topics window (Figure 4-20).*

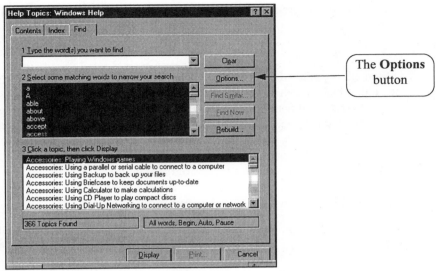

Figure 4 - 20

 PROBLEM SOLVER: *If this is the first time anyone has used Help/Find on this computer, the Find Setup wizard will appear (see Figure 4-21). This wizard sets up the database for **Find** searches. Make sure the **Minimize database size** radio button is selected, and then click on the **Next** button. The next screen tells you the process takes a while. Click on the **Finish** button and the database will be formed.*

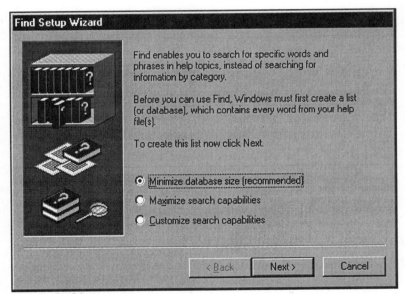

Figure 4 - 21

5. Click on the **Options** button (see Figure 4-20) and in the **Find Options** dialog box click on the **All the words...** button and change any other options until your screen resembles Figure 4-22.

6. Click on **OK** to return to the **Find** panel.

7. At the **Find** panel, type the words **file manager** in the text box labeled **Type the word(s) you want to find**.

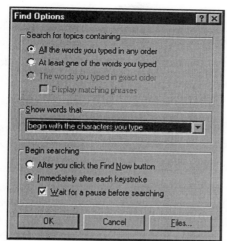

Figure 4 - 22

8. At the part of the panel labeled: **Click a topic....** ,click on: **If you've used Windows before: answers to common questions**, and then click on **Display**.

   A Windows Help window appears with answers to common questions.

9. Maximize the Windows Help window so that you will be able to read the answer to the question you will select.

10. Click on the **What happened to File Manager?** button.

    *The answer to **What happened to File Manager?** is listed on the right side of the window with an illustration below the text (Figure 4-23). The new File Manager in Windows 95 is called Windows Explorer. You will learn about the Windows Explorer in Lesson 7.*

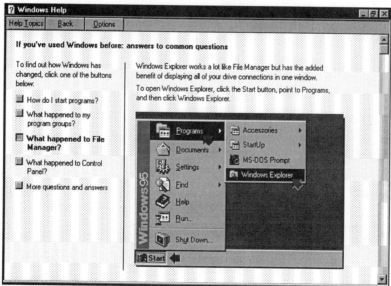

Figure 4 - 23

11. Click on the **Restore** button in the Windows Help window to restore it to its previous size.

12. Click on the **Help Topics** button below the Title bar to return to the **Find** tab.

    Now, you will change the Find options to see if you can find any more help regarding file management, the File Manager, or Windows Explorer.

13. Click on the **Options** button.

    *The **Find Options** dialog box appears (see Figure 4-22).*

14. Select **At least one of the words you typed** from the *Search for Topics* area.

15. Select **contain the characters you type** from the *Show Words* area.

16. Click on **OK**.

    *You will return to the **Find** tab. Notice the change in Find options listed at the bottom of the window. Now listed are: **One+ words, Containing, Auto, Pause**.*

17. Type **file manager** in the first text box, if it is not already there.

    *Rather than several topics (1 or 2), there are many (148 or 158). The number will vary depending on how Windows 95 was installed on your computer. The list now contains all the topics that contain **either** the word **File** or the word **Manager.***

18. Scroll down the list until you see **Formatting a disk** and click on it.

    Formatting a disk is a typical operation found in File Manager in Windows 3.1.

19. Click on **Display**.

    A Windows Help window appears with help for formatting a disk. Directions for formatting a disk are given using My Computer.

20. Keep this Windows Help window open for the next activity.

PRINTING HELP TOPICS

To keep a permanent record of your successful searches, you may want to print out the Help topics you use.

To print a Help topic:

- Display the Help topic using any of the search methods: **Contents** tab, **Index** tab, or **Find** tab.
- Click on the **Options** button under the Title bar.
- Click on **Print Topic** from the menu that appears.

    *The **Print** dialog box appears on the screen.*

- Select any options, and then click on **OK**.

Activity 4.5: Printing a Help Topic

In this activity you will print a copy of the Windows Help window for formatting a disk which you opened in the last activity.

1. After Activity 4.4, the **Windows Help** window for formatting a disk should be on the screen. If it is not, open **Help**, click on the **Find** tab and follow steps 13-19 in Activity 4.4.

2. Maximize the Windows Help window.

    Your screen will resemble Figure 4-24.

3. Click on the **Options** button under the Title bar.

    *A submenu appears on top of the **Options** button (Figure 4-25).*

4. Click on **Print Topic**.

    *The **Print** dialog box appears (Figure 4-26).*

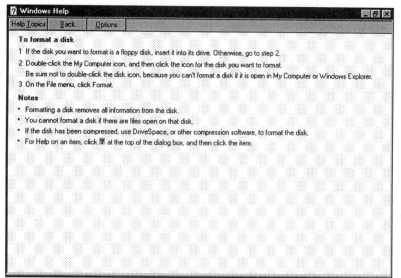

Figure 4 - 24

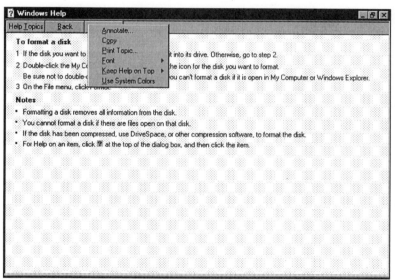

Figure 4 - 25

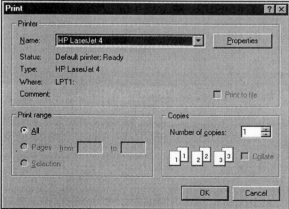

Figure 4 - 26

5.   Make sure your printer appears in the **Name** list box, and then click on **OK**.

A message appears on the screen indicating that "Formatting a disk" is being printed.

6.   Close the Windows Help window.

You will return to the Desktop.

SUMMARY

Help is extensive and accessible throughout *Windows 95*. In Lesson 4, you learned how to access Help using the **Start** menu, the **Help** button in a dialog box, and the right mouse button. Within the Help feature, the **Contents**, **Index**, and **Find** tabs were used to find help in different ways. The **Contents** tab was used to see Help subjects listed hierarchically. The **Index** tab was used to see an alphabetical listing of topics. The **Find** tab was to search for a word or phrase rather than a topic.

KEY TERMS

Closed Book	Help Button	Open Book
Contents Tab	Help Topics	Print Topic
Find Tab	Index Tab	What's This?

INDEPENDENT PROJECTS

The four independent projects will allow you to practice the basic skills involved in using the Help features in *Windows 95*.

You will practice accessing Help by using the **Help** button and the right mouse button (Independent Project 4.1), using the **Contents** tab (Independent Project 4.2), using the **Index** tab (Independent Project 4.3), and using the **Find** tab (Independent Project 4.4).

Independent Project 4.1: Accessing Help Using Shortcut Methods

In this project, you will open a Control Panel program you have not yet seen, and you will get Help for it using both the Help button and the right mouse button. The quick pop-up explanations or definitions you get will not have a Print command available, so you will use the Print Screen method to create a permanent record of them.

1.   Open the Control Panel window.

2.   Open one of the following Control programs which you haven't investigated yet, such as **Multimedia**.

3.   Click the **Help** button, and then click on a part of the dialog box you do not understand.

*Help will appear in a pop-up box above the item you selected. You will print a picture of the screen using the **Print Screen** button and WordPad. This process is described in Lesson 2.*

4.   Make sure the **Help** pop-up box is still on the screen, and then press the **Print Screen** button.

5.   Click on the **Start** button, point to **Programs**, then **Accessories**, and then click on **WordPad**.

6.   On the *WordPad* screen, type your name and the current date, and then press **ENTER** twice.

7.   Choose **EDIT/Paste**.

A picture of the screen will appear.

8.   **Print** the document.

9. **Close** WordPad. When asked if you wish to save your changes, answer **No**.

10. Minimize *WordPad*.

    You will return to the Control Panel program which you had open before you started printing.

11. **Close** the program you opened in Step 2 (probably **Multimedia**).

12. Double-click on another icon in the Control Panel window, for example **Sounds**.

13. Point to a part of the dialog box you do not understand.

14. Click the *right mouse button.*

    A pop-up menu will appear.

16. Choose **What's This?**

    A definition or explanation of the selected item will appear.

17. Use the Print Screen method as you did earlier in this project to create a printout of the screen with the **Help** pop-up. Make sure your name and the date appears on the printout.

    HINT: *WordPad should be minimized. Click on the WordPad button on the Taskbar to restore the program before you paste the new image from the Clipboard.*

18. Close *WordPad* without saving the document.

19. Close all the open windows on your Desktop.

Independent Project 4.2: Accessing Help Using the Contents Tab

In this project you will get Help for troubleshooting common problems. This is a useful feature of *Windows 95* Help. If you are having trouble with a *Windows 95* feature in the future, try these troubleshooting Help files first before making a phone call to Microsoft.

1. Open **Help** from the **Start** menu.

2. Click on the **Contents** tab.

3. Double-click on the Troubleshooting topic.

    You can double-click on the text or the closed book icon.

4. Double-click on **If you have trouble printing**.

    Each of the Troubleshooting Help documents directs you through a series of questions to help you solve the problem.

5. Print the first screen of the Troubleshooting file, using the **Options** button.

6. Click on the gray buttons as if you were experiencing the problem.

7. Close the Help window.

Independent Project 4.3: Accessing Help Using the Index Tab

In this project you will access Help for the **Windows Explorer** using the **Index** tab. You will learn about the **Explorer** in Lesson 7. After accessing the Help window, you will print out the Help information.

1. Open **Help** from the **Start** menu.

2. Click on the **Index** tab.

3. Type **Windows Explorer** in the text box labeled, *Type the first few letters of the word you're looking for*.

4. Double-click on one of the subtopics.

5. Print the Help topic, and close the Help window.

Independent Project 4.4: Accessing Help Using the Find Tab

In this project you will access Help for the concept of **hierarchies** used in organizing the folders and documents on your computer. Lesson 7 will explain the concept of hierarchies more fully. Here, you will use the **Find** index tab to get the Help information you need. After accessing the Help window, you will print out the Help information.

1. Open **Help** from the **Start** menu.

2. Click on the **Find** tab.

3. Type **hierarchy** in the text box labeled, *Type the word(s) you want to find*.

    Hierarchy is the only word that appears in the matching list, so there is no need to click anything in that list box. At least two topics appear in the bottom list box: Seeing what's on your computer and Viewing the hierarchy of folders on a disk drive.

4. Open one of these topics.

5. Print the topic, and then close the Help window.

5 Using WordPad

Objectives

In this lesson you will learn how to:

- Create a basic word processing document
- Select text
- Move the cursor

- Perform basic editing functions
- Format text
- Print multiple copies of a document

PROJECT: CREATING A BASIC DOCUMENT USING WORDPAD

In Lesson 2, you learned to create, save and print simple documents using *WordPad*, the word processing program included with *Windows 95*. In this lesson, you will learn more about using the features of WordPad to select, edit and format text. Even though you may not plan to use WordPad as your primary word processor, the tasks you accomplish in this lesson may be applied to all programs that work with text in the *Windows 95* environment. There will be minimal differences between how you perform these tasks in *WordPad* and in other programs.

WHAT IS WORDPAD?

WordPad is one of the programs found in the group of Accessories included with *Windows 95*. You have already used it in Lesson 2 to prepare your data disk. *WordPad* is a simple word processing application that replaces *Windows Write*, which was included with earlier versions of *Windows*. If your word processing needs are basic —creating simple documents *without* advanced features such as graphics, tables, print preview, spell check, and thesaurus — then WordPad may be useful to you.

RUNNING WORDPAD

WordPad is found at the bottom of the list of Accessories. The Accessories list is reached through the Programs command on the **Start** menu.

REMEMBER: *Read the bulleted list that follows, but do not actually perform the steps until you reach Activity 5.1.*

To run WordPad:

- Click on the **Start** button.
- Point to **Programs**.
- Point to **Accessories**, and then click on **WordPad**.

  The WordPad *window will open (see Figure 5-1).*

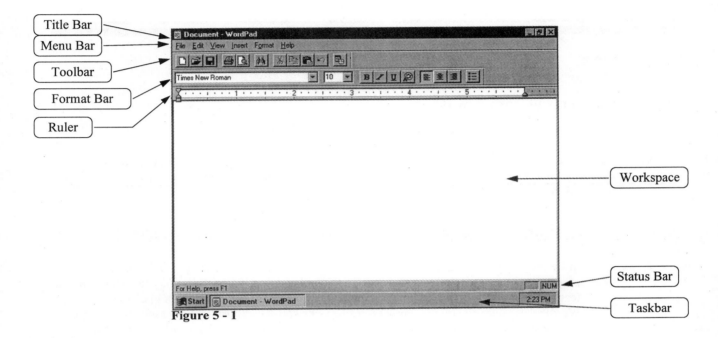

Figure 5 - 1

Activity 5.1: Opening WordPad

1. Turn on your computer.
2. To open WordPad, at the Desktop, click on the **Start** button.
3. Point to **Programs**.
4. Point to **Accessories**, and then click on **WordPad**.

   The WordPad window will open (see Figure 5-1).
5. Maximize the WordPad window.
6. Insert your data disk into the floppy drive of your computer.
7. Leave WordPad running for the next activity.

THE WORDPAD SCREEN

As you saw in Lesson 2, the WordPad screen contains many elements that are common to all windows programs (see Figure 5-1).

Before using WordPad there are certain options that you should set. Then, in Activity 5.2, you will type a letter requesting information about an interesting summer program. If you make any mistakes while typing, you may correct them by pressing the **BACKSPACE** key and retyping. Later in the lesson, you will practice editing procedures for inserting and deleting text.

Setting the View Options in WordPad

Like other *Windows 95* programs, WordPad may be set to display or hide certain screen elements. These elements are listed on the **View** menu (see Figure 5-2).

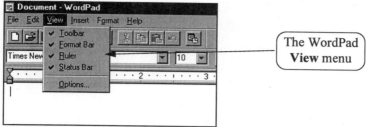

Figure 5 - 2

The **View** menu also lets you set *word wrap*. Word wrap is a feature common to all word processors. It allows you to type to the end of a line and then automatically move down to the left margin of the next line.

To view or hide elements of the WordPad screen:

- Click on the **View** menu.

- To see an element of the screen that is hidden, or to hide one that is currently displayed, click on the name of the feature (for example, **Ruler**).

  Screen elements will be checked when they are displayed and will be unchecked when they are hidden.

To turn on word wrap:

- Click on **VIEW/Options** at the menu.

- Click on the index tab for the format in which you want to save the documents you create.

- Click on the button marked **Wrap to ruler**.

- Click on **OK**.

Activity 5.2: Creating and Saving a basic document

In this activity you will create a document using WordPad and set options and display elements of the WordPad screen.

1. Open WordPad, if it is not already running.

2. Maximize the WordPad window, if it is not already maximized.

3. Click on the **View** menu.

   *You will see the following parts of the screen listed: **Toolbar**, **Format Bar**, **Ruler**, and **Status Bar**. To display these elements on the screen, each must be checked.*

4. Click on any of these words that is not checked (see Figure 5-2).

   *You may have to open the menu more than once. When you are done your **View** menu should look like the one in Figure 5-2.*

5. Open the **View** menu again and click on **Options**.

6. Click on the **Word 6** index tab.

7. Click the button in front of the words: **Wrap to ruler**

8. Click on **OK**.

   This will set word wrap properly.

9. Type the following letter in WordPad.

   o   Press **ENTER** at the end of any line which does not reach the right margin.

   o   Press **ENTER** to skip a line.

   o   While you are typing the two paragraphs of the letter, do **NOT** press **ENTER** until you reach the end of the paragraph.

   o   After typing the second paragraph, press **ENTER** twice and type **Sincerely yours,** after which you may press **ENTER** three times and type the signature.

   o   When you finish, scroll up to the beginning of the letter and compare your screen to Figure 5-3.

   NOTE: *Lines will wrap at different spots on different computers. Do **NOT** press **ENTER** to get your lines to wrap exactly as they do in Figure 5-3 or below.*

January 12, 1997

Ms. Marion Lange
Summer Abroad Program
Hudson University
Rhinebeck, New York 12572

Dear Ms. Lange:

I am interested in the summer abroad program offered by Hudson University called Students on the Move. I saw an announcement about the program at our Student Center and think it might fit my needs. I would like to spend part of the summer studying in London, and the rest of the summer traveling through England, Ireland, and Scotland. I would like to know the requirements for participating. My field of interest is English History and I am also interested in geology.

Please send me complete information on your program as soon as it is available. Please mail to Karen Venner, 12 Bailey Hall, Carmon College, Dayton, Ohio 45390. If you prefer, you may send e-mail to klv99@carmon.edu. Thank you very much.

Sincerely yours,

Karen Venner

10. To save the document, at the Menu Bar, click on **FILE/Save As** or click the **Save** button on the WordPad Toolbar.

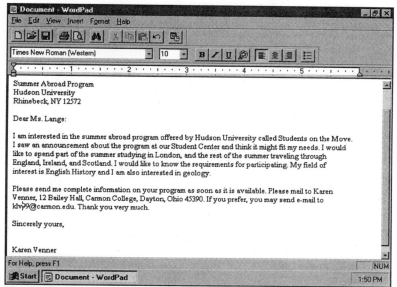

Figure 5 - 3

 PROBLEM SOLVER: *If the toolbar is not visible, click on* ***VIEW/Toolbar***.

11. In the **Save As** dialog box, type: **summer travel** as the file name (see Figure 5-4).

If the documents have file extensions (.doc), they may be hidden. Return to the Desktop by Restoring or Minimizing WordPad and open the My Computer window. Choose VIEW/Options, click on the View index tab, and check the box marked: Hide MS-DOS file extensions.....Click on ***OK***. *Then, close the* ***My Computer*** *window and Restore WordPad.*

12. In the **Save in:** box, make sure the drive listed is the one containing your data disk. The files listed are the ones you created in Lesson 2.

13. If necessary, change the type of document to **Word for Windows 6.0**.

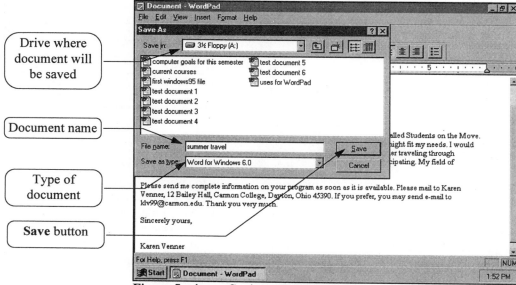

Figure 5 - 4   Saving a Document

14. Click the **Save** button to save the document.

15. Leave the document open for the next activity.

MOVING THE CURSOR

As you completed Activity 5.2, you probably noticed the blinking vertical *cursor* moving as you typed. The cursor, also known as the *insertion point*, may appear before, after, or between characters. It shows the *active position* in the document—the spot where text will be added or deleted. A person doing word processing should always be aware of the location of the cursor.

To edit a document, first position the cursor at a specific location. You may move the cursor with the mouse or the keyboard. When using the keyboard, you will move the mouse with the four gray arrow keys found between the keyboard and the numeric keypad.

When using the mouse, be sure you are able to differentiate between the cursor and the mouse pointer. The cursor is the vertical bar on your screen that blinks (except when it is moving), and the mouse pointer is the slender I you see as you slide the mouse over the workspace.

To move the cursor using the mouse:

- Position the mouse pointer in the exact location where you would like to move the cursor.

  Bring the mouse very close to the text. You must be able to see the I shape for the mouse; if the mouse pointer is an arrow, you will highlight text when you click.

- Click the left mouse button.

  The cursor will jump to the location your mouse pointer occupied when you clicked.

- Move the mouse out of the way so that you can see the cursor clearly.

To move the cursor using the keyboard:

One character to the right	Right arrow key →
One character to the left	Left arrow key ←
One line down	Down arrow key ↓
One line up	Up arrow key ↑
One word to the right	CTRL + →
One word to the left	CTRL + ←
Beginning of the line	HOME
End of the line	END
Beginning of the document	CTRL + HOME
End of the document	CTRL + END

Table 5 - 1

EDITING THE DOCUMENT

The most powerful feature of any word processor is its ability to insert new text into a document and delete unwanted text. Because all word processors perform these functions in much the same way, you will be able to apply the following instructions to any word processor you use in the *Windows 95* environment. Inserting text involves positioning the cursor and then typing the new text into the document. Deleting text may be done with either the **DELETE** or **BACKSPACE** key, depending on where the cursor is in relation to the text to be deleted. The **DELETE** key, found one row above and to the right of the main **ENTER** key, will remove the character directly following the blinking cursor. The **BACKSPACE** key, found two rows above the **ENTER** key, will remove the character that directly precedes the cursor.

To insert new text into a document:

- Position the blinking cursor at the point in the document where the new text should go.
- Type the text.

CAUTION: *Do **NOT** press the **Insert** key, or you will replace existing text with the new text you type*

To delete text using the Delete key:

- Position the blinking cursor to the left of the text you wish to delete.
- Tap the **DELETE** key once for each character, space, or punctuation mark you wish to delete.

To delete text using the Backspace key:

- Position the blinking cursor to the right of the text you wish to delete.
- Tap the **BACKSPACE** key once for each character, space, or punctuation mark you wish to delete.

Activity 5.3: Moving the Cursor and Editing Text

1. Position your mouse pointer just past the **m** of **program** in the first sentence and click to move the cursor there (see Figure 5-5).

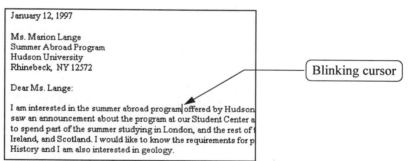

Figure 5 - 5

PROBLEM SOLVER: *If the text is highlighted and the cursor disappeared, you did not keep the mouse from moving as you clicked. Press one of the arrow keys to remove the highlighting and try this step again.*

2. Type the following text: **, including possible financial assistance,**

3. Use the gray arrow keys to position your cursor in front of the **C** of **Carmon College** in paragraph 2.

4. Type the following text: **Room 206,**

    Be sure to add the necessary spaces and punctuation.

5. Position your cursor in front of the **I** of **Ireland** in paragraph 1 of the letter.

    You may use either the mouse or the keyboard to move your cursor.

6. Use the **DELETE** key to delete the word **Ireland** and the comma and space that follow.

7. Position the cursor in front of the word **at** in the second sentence of paragraph 1.

8. Use the **DELETE** key to delete the words: **at our Student Center**

9. Correct the spacing.

10. Position the cursor in front of the period at the end of paragraph 1.

11. Use the **BACKSPACE** key to delete the words: **and I am also interested in geology**

12. Make sure that the period ends what is left of the sentence by deleting the space between **History** and the period.

13. Leave your letter onscreen for the next activity. Your letter should resemble Figure 5-6.

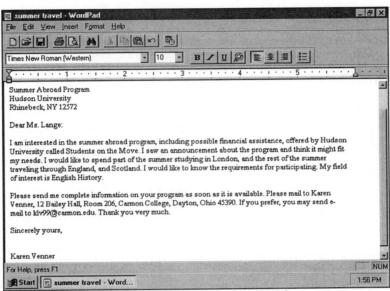

Figure 5 - 6   Summary Travel after Activity 5.3

SAVING YOUR CHANGES AND PRINTING THE DOCUMENT

There is a difference between saving a document for the first time, as you did in Lesson 2, and re-saving a document. When you resave a document, the document already has a name and you are actually replacing the original saved file with the latest version that includes all your changes. To do this you use the **FILE/Save** command. When you click on **FILE/Save**, no dialog box will open, since there is no need to give new or additional information to the computer. If you prefer, you may click on the **Save** button on the Toolbar.

To print the document, you will click the **Print** button on the toolbar or click on **FILE/Print** at the menu. As before, these are basic commands that you can use with virtually all programs designed for the *Windows* environment.

To re-save a document without changing its name:

- Click on **FILE/Save** at the menu.
- If you prefer, you may click the **Save** button ![save icon] on the toolbar.

To print a document:

- Click on **FILE/Print** at the menu.
- At the **Print** dialog box, click on **OK**.
- If you prefer, you may click on the **Print** button ![print icon] on the toolbar.

Activity 5.4: Saving and printing the letter

1. To save the letter with your changes, click on **FILE/Save** at the menu.

2. To print the letter, click on the **Print** button on the toolbar.

3. Leave the letter onscreen for the next activity.

SELECTING TEXT

It is possible that you felt annoyed as you repeatedly pressed the **DELETE** or **BACKSPACE** key in Activity 5.3 to delete one character at a time. You may have wondered if there was a way to delete a block of text as a single unit. To do so, you will learn to *select*, or highlight text. When text is selected, WordPad (or any other word processor) will treat the selected text as a unit, and any action performed will affect the entire selection. Once text is selected, it can be deleted, moved, copied, and formatted easily. You may use the mouse or the keyboard to select text.

To select text using the mouse:

Select a **single word**	Double-click on the word.
Select a **line**	Position the mouse pointer in the left margin, point to the line and click.
Select a **paragraph**	Triple-click on the paragraph (lightly).
Select a **block of text**	Click at the beginning of the block, then press down the **Shift** key and click at the end of the block. If the block ends in the middle of a word, WordPad will select the text through the end of the word.
Select any amount of text	Position the mouse pointer at the beginning of the text, hold the mouse button down and drag the mouse across the text to be selected.

Table 5 - 2

To select text using the keyboard:

Select to end of word	CTRL+SHIFT+RIGHT ARROW
Select to end of paragraph	CTRL+SHIFT+DOWN ARROW
Select to end of document	CTRL+SHIFT+END
Select a block of text	Position cursor at start of block, hold down SHIFT and use arrow keys to highlight the block
Select entire document	CTRL+5 (keypad)

Table 5 - 3

To unselect text:

- Click on text anywhere in the workspace, or tap one of the gray arrow keys.

Activity 5.5: Selecting text

1. Your letter should still be open. Use **CTRL+HOME** to move to the top.

2. To select the word **Scotland** in paragraph 1, position the mouse pointer on the word and lightly double-click (see Figure 5-7).

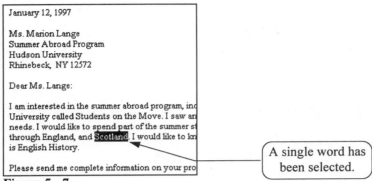

January 12, 1997

Ms. Marion Lange
Summer Abroad Program
Hudson University
Rhinebeck, NY 12572

Dear Ms. Lange:

I am interested in the summer abroad program, inc
University called Students on the Move. I saw an
needs. I would like to spend part of the summer st
through England, and Scotland. I would like to kn
is English History.

Please send me complete information on your pro

A single word has been selected.

Figure 5 - 7

3. To select the word **Ohio** in paragraph 2, position the mouse pointer on the word and double-click.

   *This will select **Ohio** and remove the selection from **Scotland**. Only 1 block of text at a time may be selected.*

4. To select the first line of the letter (**I am interested...**), position the mouse pointer in the left margin area, point to the line and click.

5. To select all of paragraph 1, position your mouse pointer anywhere on the first paragraph and triple-click. Remember to click lightly so the clicks will register properly (see Figure 5-8).

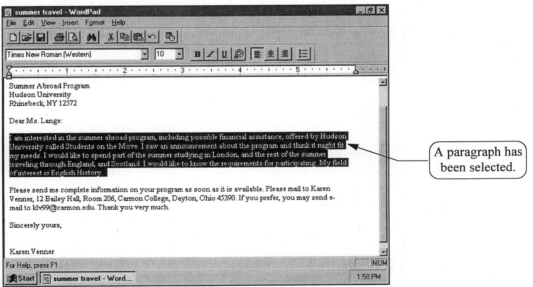

A paragraph has been selected.

Figure 5 - 8

6. Unselect the paragraph by clicking anywhere in the text.

7. To select a block of text in paragraph 2:

   o Click the mouse in front of the word **complete**.

   o Holding down the **SHIFT** key, click after the word **program**.

8. To select all of paragraph 2, position the mouse just at the beginning of the paragraph, hold the mouse button down and drag the mouse across the text you want to select.

9. Unselect the paragraph.

10. To select the line reading **Dear Ms. Lange**, using the keyboard:

    o Use the gray arrow keys to position the cursor in front of the word **Dear**.

    o Holding down the **SHIFT** key, tap the right arrow until the line is selected.

11. To select paragraph 2 using the keyboard:

    o Position the cursor in front of paragraph 2.

    o Use **SHIFT** plus the ↓ and → keys to highlight the entire paragraph.

12. Unselect the text.

13. Move to the top of the document with **CTRL+HOME**.

14. Make sure the numeric keypad is turned on.

    *Pressing the **Num Lock** key at the top of the numeric keypad turns it on. Most keyboards display a green light when **Num Lock** is on. If your keyboard is different, ask your instructor or lab assistant for help.*

15. To select the entire document, press **CTRL** and tap the **5** on the number keypad at the right side of your keyboard. Your document should look like Figure 5-9.

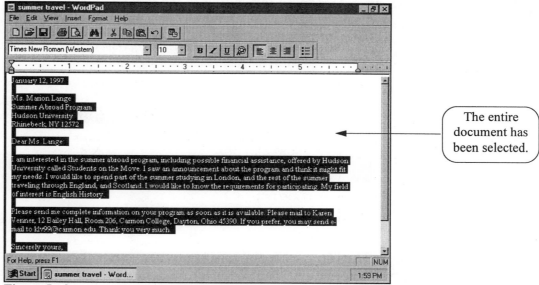

The entire document has been selected.

Figure 5 - 9

16. Unselect the text.

17. Leave the document onscreen for the next activity.

FORMATTING THE DOCUMENT

The word *formatting* means changing the appearance of all or part of a document so that it looks better and is easier to read and understand. Formatting may include adding *bold*, *italics*, and *underline* to text, changing fonts and font sizes, changing line spacing, indents, alignments, margins, and many other settings.

To make text bold:

- Select the text you want to bold.
- Click the **Bold** button **B** on the Format toolbar, or press **CTRL+B**.

To make text italicized:

- Select the text you wish to italicize.
- Click the **Italics** button *I* on the Format toolbar, or press **CTRL+I**.

To underline text:

- Select the text you want to underline.
- Click the **Underline** button **U** on the Format toolbar, or press **CTRL+U**.

To remove bold or italics from text:

- Select the text that contains the bold or italics.
- Click the **Bold**, **Italics** or **Underline** button on the Format toolbar, or press **CTRL+B**, **CTRL+I** or **CTRL+U**.

Activity 5.6: Adding formatting to the letter

1. To bold the e-mail address in paragraph 2:

    o   Select the e-mail address by clicking in front of the first character and dragging the mouse across the entire address.

    o   Click on the **Bold** button on the Formatting toolbar (see Figure 5-10).

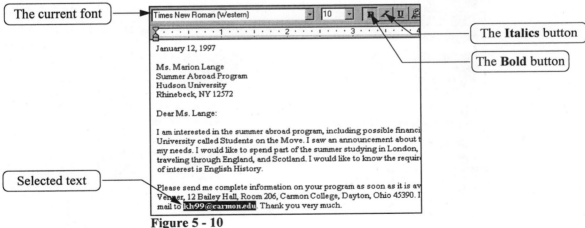

Figure 5 - 10

    o   Click elsewhere in the document to remove the selection.

2. To italicize the name of the summer program:

    o   Select the words *Students on the Move* using the **SHIFT** key and the gray arrow keys.

    o   Click the **Italics** button on the Format toolbar.

3. At the Menu Bar, click on **FILE/Save** to save your changes.

4. Leave the document onscreen for the next activity. Your screen should resemble Figure 5-11.

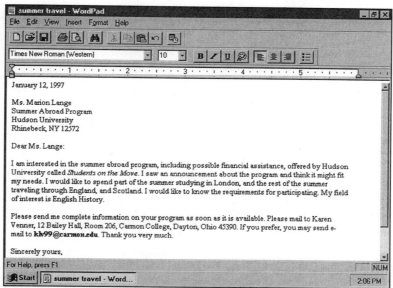

Figure 5 - 11   Summer Travel after Activity 5.6

MOVING AND COPYING TEXT

You use the same techniques for selecting text when you want to move or copy parts of your document. The process for moving text is called *Cut and Paste.* Once you have selected the text you want to move you first cut, or remove it temporarily from the document, and then paste it into a new location.

The process for copying text is called *Copy and Paste.* To copy text, first select it, then copy it, and finally paste it into the new location. Copied or moved text resides in the *Windows* Clipboard, and may be pasted more than once.

To move text:

- Select the text to be moved.
- Click the **Cut** button ✄ on the toolbar, or click on **EDIT/Cut** at the menu.
- Move the cursor to the location where the text will go.
- Click the **Paste** button on the toolbar, or click on **EDIT/Paste** at the menu.

To copy text:

- Select the text to be copied.
- Click the **Copy** button on the toolbar, or click on **EDIT/Copy** at the menu.
- Move the cursor to the location where the text will go.
- Click the **Paste** button on the toolbar, or click on **EDIT/Paste** at the menu.

Activity 5.7: Moving and copying text

1. To move the sentence reading: **I would like to know the requirements for participating.** from paragraph 1 to paragraph 2:

    o   Select the sentence by positioning the cursor in front of the sentence, holding down the **SHIFT** key, and tapping the → until the entire sentence, including the period, is selected.

    o   Click the **Cut** button on the toolbar (see Figure 5-12).

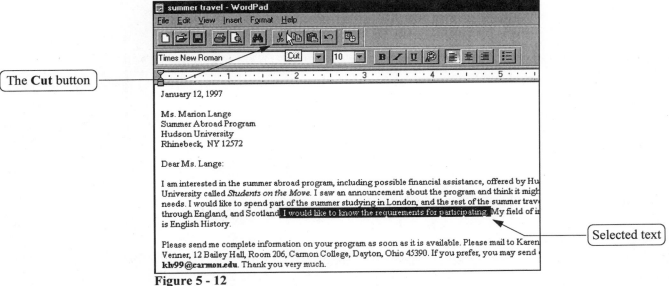

Figure 5 - 12

- o Move the cursor to paragraph 2 by positioning the mouse in front of the **P** that begins the paragraph. **Make sure you see the I pointer**, and then click..

- o Click the **Paste** button on the toolbar.

- o If necessary, put a space between the sentence you just moved and the next sentence of paragraph 2 (see Figure 5-13).

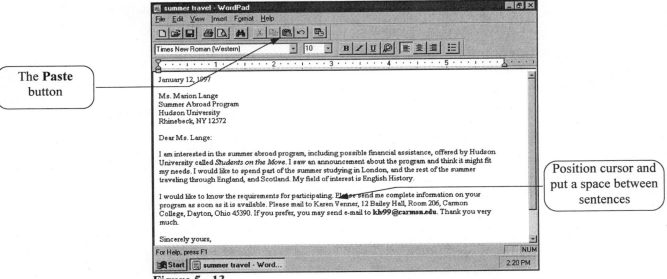

Figure 5 - 13

2. To copy Karen's name and address to the top of the letter:

- o Select her name and address by clicking in front of the **K** of **Karen** in paragraph 2, and dragging the mouse across her entire name and address.

- o Click the **Copy** button on the toolbar.

- o Bring the cursor to the beginning of the document by pressing **CTRL+HOME**.

- o To create space at the top of the document, press **ENTER** three times.

○ Press **CTRL+HOME** again.

○ Click the **Paste** button on the toolbar. Your screen should resemble Figure 5-14.

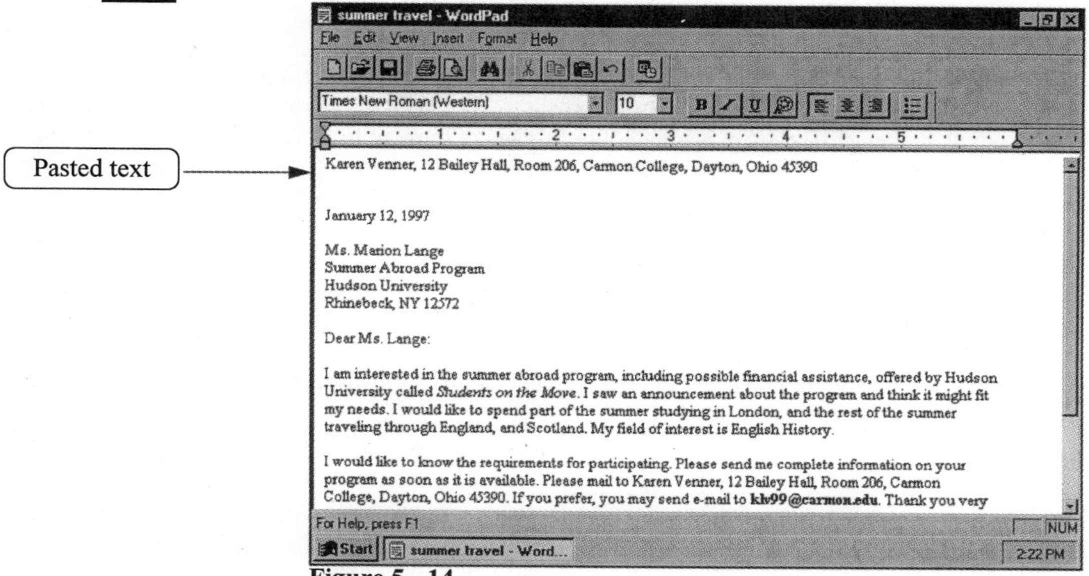

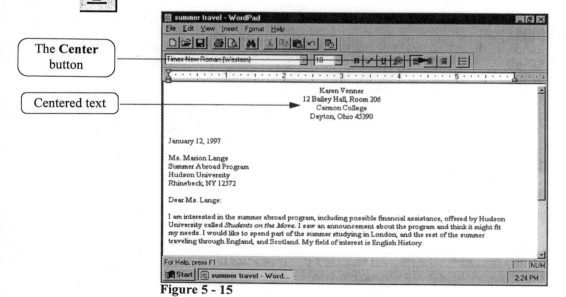

Figure 5 - 14

3. To delete the comma and space, click the mouse after the **r** of **Venner** and press **DELETE** twice.

4. Press **ENTER**.

5. Delete the comma and space after the **6** of the room number.

6. Press **ENTER**.

7. Delete the comma and space after the **e** of **College**.

8. Press **ENTER**.

9. Select all four lines.

10. To center the name and address, click the **Center** button (see Figure 5-15).

Figure 5 - 15

11. Re-save the file.

12. Leave the document onscreen for the next activity.

PRINTING MULTIPLE COPIES OF THE DOCUMENT

When you click the **Print** button on the toolbar you print a single copy of the document that is onscreen. The advantage of taking an extra moment to click on **FILE/Print** at the menu is that the dialog box that opens offers extra printing options. One of these options is the ability to print more than one copy of the document. In the last activity of this project, we will print two copies of our letter. As before, the **FILE/Print** option is so basic that you can use it with virtually all programs designed for the *Windows* environment.

To print more than 1 copy of a document:

- Click on **FILE/Print** at the menu.

- Change the number of copies by typing in a new number or by clicking one of the arrow keys in the **Number of copies:** box.

- Click on **OK**.

Activity 5.8: Printing the Letter

1. To print two copies of the letter, click on **FILE/Print** at the menu.

2. Change the number of copies from **1** to **2** by clicking on the ↑ to the right of the number of copies (see Figure 5-16).

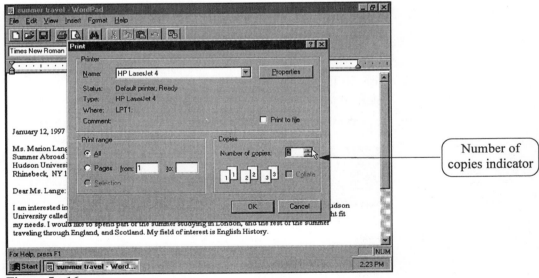

Figure 5 - 16

3. Click on **OK**.

4. Examine the copies of the letter that have printed and make any additional changes to the document onscreen that you feel are necessary.

5. Change the number of copies to print back to 1.

6. If you have made changes, save the letter again.

7. Close WordPad.

8. Shut down *Windows 95*.

SUMMARY

In this lesson, you practiced using many of the features of WordPad, the *Windows 95* word processing program. You learned to create a document, move the cursor, and edit your document by inserting new text and deleting unwanted text. Next, you learned to select, or highlight text, and format text by enhancing it with bold, italics and underline. Finally, you learned to save changes and print multiple copies of your document.

KEY TERMS

Backspace	Delete	Paste
Bold	Format	Select
Copy	Insert	Underline
Cursor	Italics	Word wrap
Cut	Mouse Pointer	Wrap to Ruler

INDEPENDENT PROJECTS

These projects will reinforce the skills you learned in Lesson 5: creating, editing, saving and printing a basic word processing document. Most of these techniques may be used with any word processing program that runs in the *Windows 95* environment.

Independent Project 5.1: Creating and Editing a Document

In this activity you will practice the skills you learned in Lesson 5. If you find that you are unable to complete this project, review the activities in Lesson 5.

1. Turn on your computer, if it is not already on.

2. Insert your data disk into the appropriate drive.

3. Run WordPad.

4. Type the following letter. Press **ENTER** at the end of any line that does not reach the right margin. Press **ENTER** when you want to leave a line blank. Do *not* press **ENTER** during the long paragraphs of the letter. Remember to type your own name as Assistant Director at the end of the letter. Be sure to note that the letter continues onto the next page. Your document should resemble Figure 5-17.

January 24, 1997

Karen Venner
12 Bailey Hall, Room 206
Carmon College
Dayton, Ohio 45390

Dear Karen:

I am enclosing information on Students on the Move. We will be offering courses at the University of London in English History, as well as a number of other subjects. The courses will be offered from July 1 through August 3. During the month of August many of the students, who come from all over the world, travel around Great Britain in informal groups. There will also be a University sponsored trip to Scotland from August 6 through August 16. We hope you will find our program to be of interest to you.

We are not able to award financial assistance, but when you read our brochure you will see that tuition is quite reasonable.

Please call me at any time if I can answer your questions or be of further assistance.

Sincerely,

Your Name, Assistant Director
Students on the Move

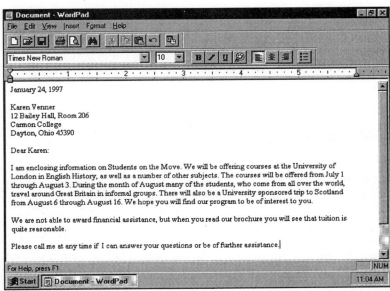

Figure 5 - 17

5. Read your document and correct any typing errors by deleting the mistakes and retyping or inserting text.

6. Add the following text to the end of the first sentence in paragraph one:

   for the summer of 1997

7. Delete **, as well as a number of other subjects** from the second sentence.

8. Change the dates of the trip to Scotland to: **August 5 through August 15**.

9. Add the following sentence to the end of paragraph two:

   In addition, low-cost charter fares will be available for the time at which you will be traveling.

10. Move the sentence: **We hope you will find our program to be of interest to you.** so that it is the last sentence of the letter.

   HINT: *Remember to select the text, click the* **Cut** *button, move the cursor and click the* **Paste** *button.*

11. Select and bold the words **Students on the Move** in the first sentence.

12. Read the document and correct any spacing or punctuation errors.

13. Save the file on your data disk as **students on the move**.

   HINT: *Be sure to change the* **Save in:** *information so that you are saving on your data disk.*

14. Print a copy of the letter.

15. Compare the printed copy to Figure 5-18 and make any further corrections that are necessary.

16. If you have made changes, resave the file and reprint the letter.

17. Close WordPad.

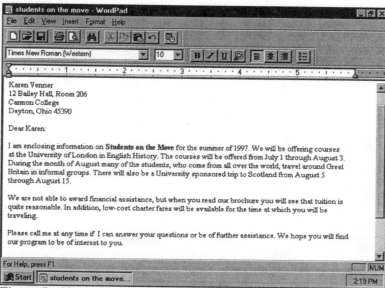

Figure 5 - 18   The Completed Document

Independent Project 5.2: Creating a Memo

In this project, you will learn to create a short memo, lining text up with the **TAB** key. This is a challenging project.

1. Turn on your computer, if it is not already on.

2. Insert your data disk into the floppy drive.

3. Run *WordPad*.

   *If WordPad is already onscreen, begin a new document by clicking on **FILE/New** at the menu. If you are asked whether you want to save changes to the document currently onscreen, remember that if you answer **No** you will lose any changes you made since the last time you saved the document.*

4. At the blank *WordPad* screen, change to **Center alignment** by clicking on the **Center** button on the Format toolbar.

5. Type: **MEMO** and make it bold.

6. Press **ENTER** twice.

7. Change back to **Left alignment** by clicking on the **Left** button on the Format toolbar.

8. Type the word **TO:** and press the **TAB** key twice. The text should not be bold.

   *The **TAB** key is found at the left of the keyboard, directly above the **CAPS LOCK** key.*

9. Type **Brett Schuman** and press **ENTER** twice.

10. Type the word **FROM:** and press **TAB** twice.

11. Type your own name, followed by a comma and **Student Travel Club**, and press **ENTER** twice.

    *You can line your text up accurately with the **TAB** key.*

12. Type the word **DATE:** and press **TAB** twice.

13. At the Menu Bar, click on **INSERT/Date and Time**.

14. Click on **OK**.

    *The current date will be inserted into your document. If the date is not correct, use the **BACKSPACE** key to remove it and then type it correctly. Remember that in Lesson 3 you learned to change the date and time at the Control Panel. You may do that after you have completed this project if the inserted date is not correct.*

15. Press **ENTER** twice.

16. Type the word **SUBJECT:** and press **TAB** *once*.

17. Type: **Spring Break Trip** and press **ENTER** twice.

18. Type: **CC:** and press **TAB** twice.

19. Type: **Michael Brewster** and press **ENTER** twice. Your screen should look like Figure 5-19.

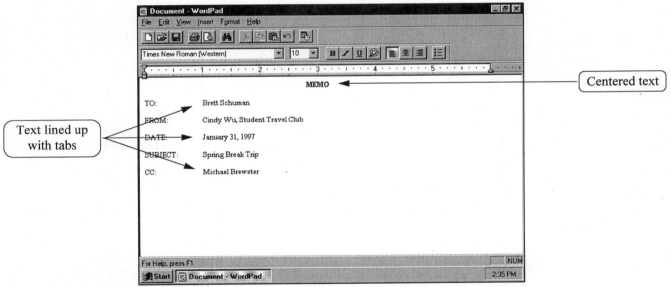

Figure 5 - 19

20. Type the next paragraph. Press **ENTER** twice at the end of the paragraph.

    I have checked prices for skiing trips and beach trips for the dates you gave me. Here is a summary of what I found. These prices are good until February 15. After that there will be an increase, but I'm not sure how much. Call me at 555-7834 if you have questions, or when you are ready to book your trip.

21. Type the following line of text. Press the **TAB** key *twice* between columns. Press **ENTER** at the end of the line

    Skiing   Jackson Hole, Wyoming   Air and hotel $899

22. Type the rest of the text, pressing the **TAB** key to line up the columns. You may have to press the **TAB** key a different number of times in some locations to line up the text. Let your eye be your guide.

Skiing	**Park City, Utah**	**Air, hotel, lift passes**	**$699**
Beach	**Nassau, Bahamas**	**Air and hotel**	**$399**
Beach	**Montego Bay, Jamaica**	**Air and hotel**	**$439**
Beach	**San Juan, Puerto Rico**	**Air, hotel, breakfast**	**$399**

23. Read the text over and correct any errors you have made.

24. Save the file on your data disk as **spring break prices**.

25. Change the price of the trip to Utah to **$799**.

26. Move the cursor to the end of the last line (just past **$399**) and press **ENTER** to add another line.

27. Add one more trip to the list:

Beach	**Cancun, Mexico**	**Air and hotel**	**$349**

28. Move both of the skiing vacations so that they are listed *below* the beach vacations. Your document should look like Figure 5-20.

   HINT: *Select and then Cut the text to be moved. Position your cursor at the end of the document and press ENTER to create a new line. Then, Paste the text.*

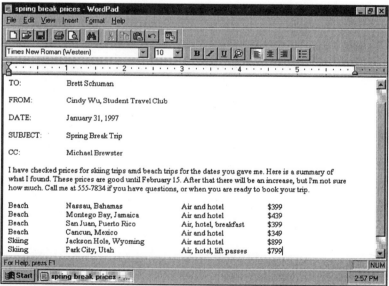

Figure 5 - 20   The Completed Document

29. Resave the file.

30. Print a single copy of the memo and proofread it.

31. Make any changes that are necessary and resave if you have made changes.

32. Print **2** copies of the memo.

33. Close WordPad.

Independent Project 5.3: Creating your own document

This last project lets you work on your own, pulling together many of the skills you learned. In addition, you will underline text, a concept explained in the lesson, but not practiced.

1. Using WordPad, write a letter to a friend you have not seen in awhile.

2. In the letter, include examples of bold, underlined and italicized text.

3. Proofread the letter, and correct any mistakes you have made.

4. Save the letter on your data disk as **myletter 1**.

5. Print a copy of the letter.

6. Revise the letter, deleting some text and adding other text.

7. Save the revised letter as a second document on your data disk, calling it **myletter 2**.

8. Print a copy of the revised letter.

9. Close WordPad.

10. Shut down *Windows 95*.

Exploring Windows 95 Accessories

Objectives

In this lesson you will learn how to:

- Understand the accessories available in *Windows 95*
- Use the *Character Map*

- Use the *Clipboard Viewer*
- Use WordPad and *Paint* to share data

A LISTING OF WINDOWS 95 ACCESSORIES

Now that you are able to use WordPad, learning to use the remaining *Windows 95* accessories will be much easier. These simple-to-use programs are designed to make your daily routines faster and more efficient. Many are electronic versions of the usual conveniences found on every desk. Although each accessory fills a different need, the basic techniques for using the accessories are the same *Windows* techniques you learned in Lesson 2 and practiced again in Lesson 5.

This lesson will introduce you to several of the accessories. For complete information about each, refer to the *Windows 95* on-line documentation. Table 6 - 1 describes important features of the accessories.

Icon	Accessory	Functions
	Calculator	• Operates in standard or scientific mode. • In standard mode performs simple calculations, percentages, and square roots. • In scientific mode performs simple scientific and statistical calculations. • In scientific mode can work in binary, octal, and hexadecimal number systems. • In statistical mode can calculate sum, sum of squares, mean, and standard deviation.
	Calendar	• *The Calendar is a Windows 3.1 accessory. You will see it only if you have upgraded to Windows 95 from Windows 3.1.* • Displays either a **Day View** or **Month View**. • Allows you to enter and display appointments for a particular day at time intervals you choose.
	Cardfile	• *The Cardfile is also a Windows 3.1 accessory. You will see it only if you have upgraded to Windows 95 from Windows 3.1.* • Can create one or more files of individual "cards," which are automatically alphabetized by the first word on the index line.
	Character Map	• Can insert special characters not on the keyboard into documents created in *Windows* applications. • Can select a font for use in *Windows* applications.
	Clipboard Viewer	• *Clipboard Viewer may not have been automatically installed. You may need to use **Add/Remove Programs** in Control Panel to install the Clipboard accessory to your computer.* • *If Windows 95 is installed on a computer that originally had Windows for Workgroups installed, the Clipboard Viewer will be called the Clipbook Viewer.* • Can view objects that have been copied or cut and thus placed on the clipboard. • Can save clipboard contents as documents for later use. • Can display contents of clipboard in different formats. • Can copy text from an MS-DOS window.
	Notepad	• Provides a simple environment in which you can take notes, jot down ideas, etc. • Can word wrap (optional). • Can search for text. • Can copy/move text to other applications.
	Paint	• Can create color drawings. • Can size the drawing for display. • Offers a selection of drawing tools for different effects in creating pictures and text. • Can select an area of the drawing, called a cutout, and work with that separately. • Can create custom colors. • Can print part of or an entire drawing.
	Phone Dialer	• Can place phone calls from your computer by using your modem.

Table 6 - 1

THE CHARACTER MAP

The *Character Map* is an accessory used to insert characters not found on most keyboards into your documents. All available characters in a particular "*font style*" are displayed on the *Character Map*. A font style is a creative design for text. Each font style has its own personality and can add interest and emphasis to your documents. The **Symbol** and **Wingdings** font styles made by *True Type* are symbol fonts; they display special symbols instead of the alphabet. For example, the π (pi) is a character found in the **Symbol** font style and the ⌨ (keyboard) is a small picture found in the **Wingdings** font style.

The fonts that are available on your machine are listed in a **Font** list box on the Format Toolbar in WordPad, and in a **Font** list box on the *Character Map*. The list will be the same in WordPad, the *Character Map* and other programs. One advantage to using the *Character Map* is that you can see all the characters available to you in one place and then insert any of the viewed characters into your document.

REMEMBER: *Read the bulleted list that follows, but do not actually perform the steps until you reach Activity 6.1.*

To open the Character Map:

- Click on the **Start** menu.
- Point to **PROGRAMS**, and then to **Accessories**.
- Click on **Character Map**.

    The Character Map window will open.

To select a font style:

- Click the ⬇ in the **Font** list box to open the list.
- Click on the desired font style.

    The characters available for the selected font style will be displayed.

To insert a character into a document:

- To see an enlarged picture of a character, point to the character in the Character Map and hold down the left mouse button.
- Click on the character you wish to insert.
- Click on **Select**.

    *A copy of the character appears in the **Characters To Copy** text box. You can select as many characters as you wish to insert into your document.*

- Click on the **Copy** button to place the selected characters onto the Clipboard.
- Switch to the document in which you want to insert the character(s).
- Position your cursor where you want to insert the character(s).
- Select the same font that was selected in the Character Map.
- Click on **EDIT/Paste**.

NOTE: *If the new font style does not take effect, highlight the character you wish to change and then click on the font style in the **Font** list box.*

Activity 6.1: Using the Character Map

In this activity you will use the *Character Map* to add symbols to a WordPad document which you created in Lesson 5. You will add the British pound character to the letter called *Students on the Move*.

1. Turn on your computer, if it is not already on.

2. Insert your data diskette into the appropriate disk drive.

3. Start WordPad, and then open the **students on the move** document from your floppy drive.

   Your screen should resemble Figure 6 - 1.

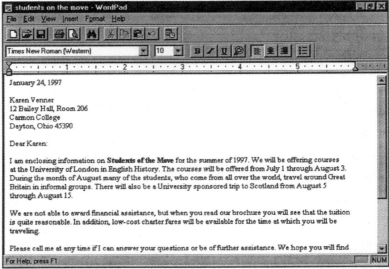

Figure 6 - 1

If you have not completed Independent Project 5.1, you will not have saved this document. If this is the case, you may use a new document.

4. Add the following paragraph after the first paragraph. Add a blank line between paragraphs, if necessary.

   For your convenience, we have arranged for special rates at several of the Inns throughout Britain. The prices listed below are for a one night stay and include breakfast.

5. Press **ENTER** twice to add a blank line and type the following columns of text.

Heathrow House	**25**
The Bird and Bottle	**30**
The Country Inn	**32**

   HINT: *Tab two times after Heathrow House. Then use the **TAB** key to line up the other numbers with the 25.*

6. Place your cursor before the **2** in **25**.

   Now, you are ready to view and copy the English Pound character from the Character Map.

7. Click on the **Start** button.

8. Point to **PROGRAMS**, and then to **Accessories**.

9. Click on **Character Map**.

    The Character Map window will open (Figure 6 - 2).

Figure 6 - 2

10. Select **Times New Roman** from the **Font** list box, if it is not already selected.

11. Find the English Pound symbol and point to it.

    HINT: *The pound symbol should be in the 5th row and the 4th column.*

12. Hold down the left mouse button to see an enlargement of the symbol (Figure 6 - 3).

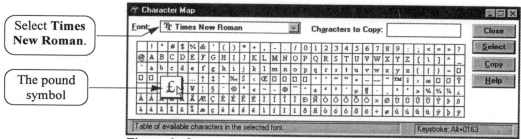

Select **Times New Roman**.

The pound symbol

Figure 6 - 3

13. Click on **Select**.

    *A copy of the character appears in the **Characters To Copy** text box (Figure 6 - 4).*

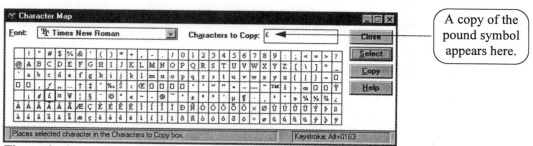

A copy of the pound symbol appears here.

Figure 6 - 4

14. Click the **Copy** button to place the Pound symbol onto the clipboard.

15. Switch back to **students on the move** by clicking on its button on the Taskbar.

16. Check to see that the cursor is still in front of the **2** in **25**, and then click on the **Paste** button in WordPad.

    The pound symbol will be inserted before the 25.

17. Press the **SPACEBAR** once to insert a space between the Pound symbol and the **25**.

    The Pound symbol will still be on the Clipboard. Therefore, you can continue to insert the symbol on the next two lines.

18. Repeat steps 15 and 16 to insert a Pound symbol and a space in front of **30** and **32**.

19. At the Menu Bar, use **FILE/Save As** to save the document on your data disk with the name: **traveling in Britain**

    The completed document will resemble Figure 6 - 5.

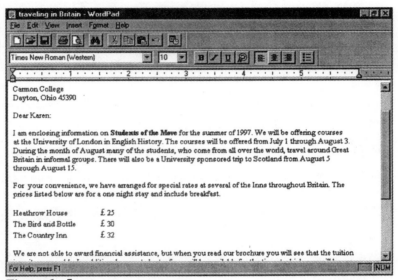

Figure 6 - 5

20. Close all the open windows.

    You will return to the Desktop.

THE CLIPBOARD VIEWER (ALSO CALLED CLIPBOOK VIEWER)

Have you wondered what happens when you *copy* or *cut* text or a picture to the Clipboard? Where does the screen image go when you press the **PRINTSCREEN** key?

    You have been told that information being cut or copied is placed on the Clipboard; however, you have never actually viewed the Clipboard contents. Now, you will use the *Clipboard Viewer* to see the cut or copied information while it is on the Clipboard.

To open the Clipboard Viewer:

- Click on the **Start** menu.

- Point to **Programs**, and then to **Accessories**.

- Click on **Clipboard Viewer** (in some cases, **Clipbook Viewer**).

    The Clipboard Viewer window will open. Whatever is currently on the clipboard will be displayed in the window.

Activity 6.2: Viewing the Clipboard

In this activity you will use the *Clipboard Viewer* to view a picture of your screen image. This kind of image is often called a *screen shot*. You will then use the screen shot in a document you will create in *WordPad*.

1. After Activity 6.1, all windows should be closed. Close any open windows, if necessary.

2. Insert your data diskette in the appropriate disk drive, if necessary.

   You will create a print screen for the Control Panel window.

3. Run the Control Panel and maximize its window.

   HINT: *Use the **Settings** menu.*

4. Press the **PRINTSCREEN** key.

   Now you will open the Clipboard Viewer and see the screen you just copied.

5. Close the Control Panel window.

6. Click on the **Start** button.

7. Point to **Programs**, then to **Accessories**, and then click on **Clipboard Viewer** (in some cases, **Clipbook Viewer**).

   The Clipboard Viewer window will open (Figure 6 - 6). The picture of the Control Panel will be displayed within the window. You will have two Title bars: one for the Clipboard Viewer and one for the Control Panel. The Control Panel is a picture, not an active window.

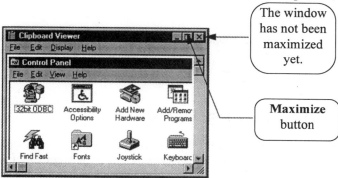

Figure 6 - 6

   PROBLEM SOLVER: *If the Clipboard Viewer has not been installed, ask your instructor or lab assistant to install it using **Add/Remove Programs** in the Control Panel.*

8. Maximize the *Clipboard Viewer* window so that you can see most of the picture. Use the scroll bars to see the whole picture.

9. Close the *Clipboard Viewer*, and then open WordPad.

   The picture of the Control Panel window will remain on the Clipboard until you copy or cut new information.

10. Type: **The Control Panel Window** on the first line of the blank WordPad document.

11. Press **ENTER** twice to add two blank lines.

12. Click on the **Paste** button on the Toolbar.

   The picture of the Control Panel will be inserted into the document (Figure 6 - 7).

PROBLEM SOLVER: *If your screen does not resemble Figure 6 - 7, you are probably looking at the end of the document. Use the vertical scroll bar to move up to the top of the document.*

Figure 6 - 7

13. Save the *WordPad* document as **The Control Panel Window** on your data disk.

14. Print the document.

15. Close *WordPad* and any other open windows.

    You will return to the Desktop.

SHARING DATA AMONG ACCESSORIES

One of the major strengths of *Windows 95* is the ease with which information can be copied or moved from one program to another. The process of moving and copying is the same regardless of whether information is being transferred within a document, within a program, or within any part of the *Windows* environment.

The *Clipboard* makes this possible. As you know, when you copy or cut information, it is placed on the *Clipboard*, which serves as a temporary holding area. As you saw in the last activity, the *Clipboard Viewer* allows you to see what is placed on the *Clipboard*. Once you have moved to the location where you want to insert the copied or cut data, you may paste the *Clipboard* contents there. This operation can be used not only with *Windows 95* accessories, but also any other program running under *Windows 95*.

To copy or move data to a different program:

- Select the data you wish to copy or move.

- Choose **EDIT/Cut** if you want to move the data, or **EDIT/Copy** if you wish to copy the data.

  The data will be transferred to the Clipboard. It will remain on the clipboard until new data takes its place.

- Run the other program, or switch to it, if it is already running.

- Position your cursor where you want the data to appear.

- Choose **EDIT/Paste** to place the data in its new location.

Activity 6.3: Sharing Data Among Accessories

In this activity you will use a new accessory, the *Notepad,* to create a document that will look as if you were taking notes during a phone conversation. Then, you will use the *Clipboard* to copy the information into WordPad, where you can make formatting changes to it.

1. After Activity 6.2 all windows should be closed.

2. Insert your data disk into the appropriate disk drive.

3. Click on the **Start** button.

4. Point to **PROGRAMS**, and then to **Accessories**.

5. Click on **Notepad**.

    The Notepad window appears on the screen (Figure 6 - 8). The Notepad is a rudimentary word processor, with fewer options than WordPad.

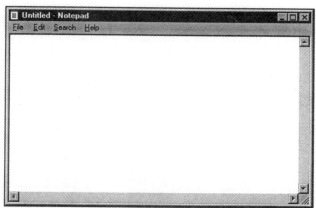

Figure 6 - 8

6. Maximize the *Notepad* window.

    Now you will type text in the Notepad as if you were taking notes during a telephone conversation.

7. Type the following information. Press **ENTER** at the end of each line. Press **ENTER** again to skip a line. If you make mistakes, use the editing techniques you learned in Lesson 5 to correct them.

    meet Joe at Mongoose Restaurant at noon on December 23
    talk about the budget for next year

    new address for Joe Jackson:
    Joe Jackson
    Executive Vice President
    National Express Bank
    50 Main Street
    Salem, MA 01970

new phone number:
(617) 555-4567

Your screen should resemble Figure 6 - 9.

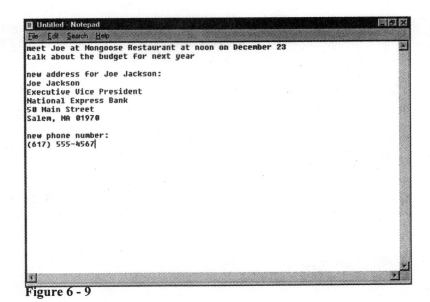

Figure 6 - 9

8. Save the *Notepad* document on your data disk as **Phone Conversation with Joe Jackson**.

9. Select Joe Jackson's name and address (Figure 6 - 10).

    Refer back to Lesson 5 for help with selecting text.

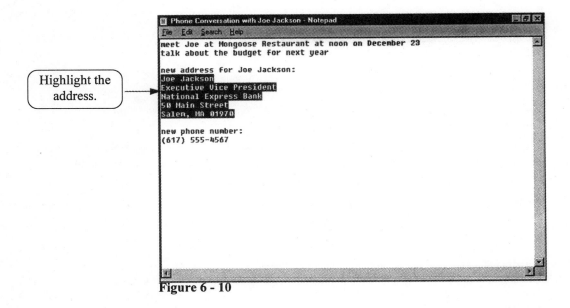

Highlight the
address.

Figure 6 - 10

10. At the Menu Bar, choose **EDIT/Copy**.

11. Minimize *Notepad*.

12. Run *WordPad*.

    You will type a letter to Joe confirming plans to have lunch.

13. At the Menu Bar, choose **INSERT/Date and Time**.

14. Click on a date format from the **Available formats** list box, and then click on **OK**.

15. Press **ENTER** four times.

16. Click on the **Paste** button on the Toolbar.

    Joe's address from the Notepad document will appear in the WordPad document (Figure 6 - 11).

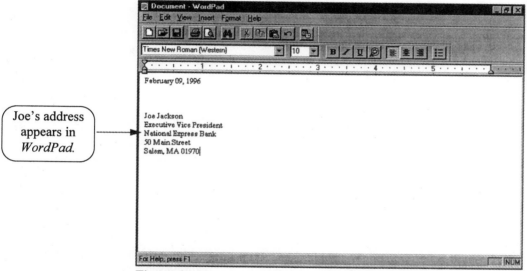

Figure 6 - 11

17. Insert **Mr.** before Joe in the address.

    Refer to Lesson 5 for help with inserting text.

18. Place your text cursor at the end of the address block, press **ENTER** twice, and then type: **Dear Joe:**

19. Again, press **ENTER** twice, and then type: **It was great talking to you today. I am looking forward to**

20. Press the **SPACEBAR** once.

21. Switch to *Notepad* by clicking on its button on the Taskbar.

22. Select the two lines that read:

    meet Joe at Mongoose Restaurant at noon on December 23

    talk about the budget for next year

21. At the Menu Bar, choose **EDIT/Copy**.

22. Switch back to *WordPad*, and then click on the **Paste** button.

    When the text is pasted, it will resemble Figure 6 - 12.

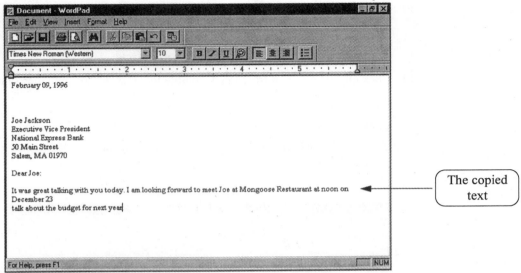

The copied text

Figure 6 - 12

23. Using the editing techniques you learned in Lesson 5, edit the current text so that the sentence reads:

    I am looking forward to meeting you for lunch at the Mongoose Restaurant on December 23 to talk about the budget for next year.

    HINT: To remove the breaks between lines, position the cursor at the end of the line preceding the break and press DELETE.

24. Press **ENTER** twice, and then type the rest of the letter as follows:

    I have had a chance to look at my schedule and a 1:00 lunch would make it easier for me to attend. I also think we should discuss next year's marketing plan as well.

    Again, I look forward to meeting with you. Call me if you have any questions or concerns at (914) 763-8778.

    Sincerely,

    (Type your name)

    The completed document will resemble Figure 6 - 13.

25. Save the document on your data disk as **Letter to Joe Jackson**.

26. Print a copy of the letter.

27. Close all the open windows.

    You will return to the Desktop.

SUMMARY

Several of the *Windows 95* accessories were explored in this lesson. You learned how to use the *Character Map* to view and insert characters into a *WordPad* document, and the *Clipboard Viewer* to view the contents of the *Clipboard*. Finally, you shared data between two accessories using *Notepad* and *WordPad*.

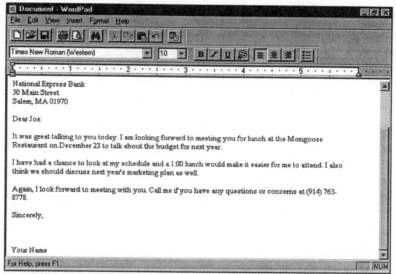

Figure 6 - 13

KEY TERMS

16 Color Bitmap	Clipboard Viewer	Paste button
Accessory	Copy button	Phone Dialer
Calculator	Cut button	Selection Tool
Calendar	Move	Text Tool
Cardfile	Notepad	Word Wrap
Character Map	Paint	

INDEPENDENT PROJECTS

The three independent projects allow you to review what you have learned and explore the *Windows 95* accessories further. In Independent Project 6.1 you will use the *Character Map* to add special characters to a document. In Independent Project 6.2, you will use the *Clipboard Viewer* to view two screen images before pasting them into *WordPad*. Finally, in Independent Project 6.3, you will share information between *Paint* and *WordPad*.

Independent Project 6.1: Using the Character Map to Add Symbols to a Document

In this project, you will use the *Character Map* to add foreign characters to a *WordPad* document.

1. Start your computer, if necessary.

2. Insert your data disk into the appropriate disk drive.

3. Run *WordPad*.

4. Display the Toolbar and Format Bar.

5. Your current font should be **Times New Roman**. If not, change to this font by opening the list of fonts on the Format Bar and clicking on it.

6. The **Font Size** (listed to the right of the Font) should be **12** points. If not, change to this font size by opening the list of sizes on the Format Bar and clicking on **12**.

7. Type the following line of text:

   Foreign Addresses for Students on the Move

8. Center align the text, by clicking on the **Center** button on the Format Bar.

9. Press **ENTER** twice.

10. Return to left alignment, by clicking on the **Align Left** button on the Format Bar.

11. Type: **France** and then press **ENTER**

12. Type the following address and press **ENTER** twice:

    122 Rue Gaspe
    Paris, France

13. Type: **Spain** and then press **ENTER**.

14. Type the following address and press **ENTER** twice:

    4 Plaza de los Ninos
    Seville, Spain

15. Type: **England** and then press **ENTER**.

16. Type the following address:

    15 Oxbridge Court
    London, England

17. Save the file as **foreign offices** on your data disk.

18. Position your cursor before the final **e** on the line that reads: **122 Rue Gaspe**.

19. To substitute the French character é, minimize WordPad.

20. Click on the **Start** button, point to **Programs**, and then **Accessories,** and run the *Character Map*.

21. Display the map for the **Times New Roman** font.

22. Look for the é symbol, and then click on it.

    The symbol should appear on the bottom row of characters.

23. Click on the **Select** button, and then on the **Copy** button.

24. Minimize the *Character Map*.

25. Restore WordPad by clicking on its button on the Taskbar.

26. Press the **DELETE** key to delete the **e** that follows the cursor.

27. Paste the é.

28. Position the cursor before the last **n** of the line that reads: **4 Plaza de los Ninos**.

29. Minimize WordPad.

30. Restore the *Character Map* by clicking on its button on the Taskbar.

31. Click on the ñ. It also appears on the bottom row of characters.

32. Click on the box labeled: **Characters to Copy:** and remove the é.

33. Click on the **Select** button, and then click on the **Copy** button.

34. Minimize the *Character Map*.

35. Restore WordPad by clicking on its button on the Taskbar.

36. Press **DELETE** to remove the **n**.

37. Paste the ñ into the document.

38. Save the document, keeping the same name.

39. Print a copy.

40. Close *WordPad*, the *Character Map*, and any other open windows.

     You will return to the Desktop.

Independent Project 6.2: Using the Clipboard Viewer

In this project, you will send two images to the *Clipboard* using the **Print Screen** button, pasting them, one at a time, into *WordPad*. You will also use the *Clipboard Viewer* to look at the pictures before you paste them into *WordPad*.

1. Insert your data disk into the appropriate disk drive.

    *You will use **PRINTSCREEN** to create pictures of the Desktop and the My Computer window.*

2. Close any open windows on the Desktop.

3. Press **PRINT SCREEN**.

4. Run the *Clipboard Viewer*, and view the image of the Desktop.

5. Minimize the *Clipboard Viewer*, and then run WordPad.

6. Type: **This is the Desktop**, press **ENTER**, and then paste the picture of the Desktop below the sentence.

7. Make sure the picture you just pasted is not selected. If necessary, click within the first sentence.

8. Minimize WordPad.

9. Double-click on the **My Computer** icon to open its window.

10. Press **PRINTSCREEN**.

11. Restore the *Clipboard Viewer* by clicking on its button on the Taskbar and look at the image of the **My Computer** window.

12. Switch to WordPad and place the text cursor at the end of the document.

13. Type a descriptive sentence for the My Computer window and then paste the picture into WordPad.

     PROBLEM SOLVER: *If the old picture disappears, it was selected when you pasted the new picture. Be sure nothing in the document is selected when you paste.*

14. Print the document.

15. Close WordPad without saving the document.

16. Exit from WordPad and *Clipboard Viewer*.

Independent Project 6.3: Sharing Data between Paint and WordPad

In this project you will create a graphic in Paint and copy it to WordPad. Paint is a *Windows 95* accessory used for drawing pictures. If you completed Independent Project 2.3 you have already worked with Paint. If not, you will be introduced to it now.

1. Start your computer, if necessary.

2. Insert your data disk into the appropriate disk drive.

3. To open Paint, click on the **Start** menu.

4. Point to **PROGRAMS**, and then **Accessories**, and then click on **Paint**.

   The Paint window will open (Figure 6 - 14). The drawing tools are displayed to the left of the drawing area. A color palette is located below the drawing area. You will draw an ellipse, and then type your name inside the ellipse.

The drawing tools

The color palette

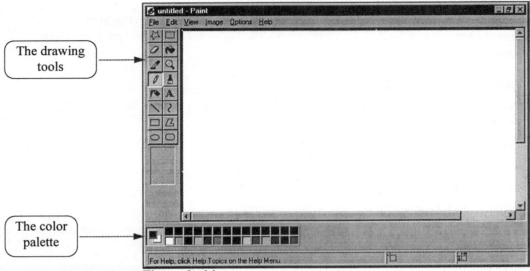

Figure 6 - 14

5. Maximize the Paint window if necessary.

6. At the Tool Box, click on the **Ellipse** tool, and then move the mouse onto the drawing area.

   The mouse changes to a cross-hair symbol.

7. To draw an ellipse in the upper left hand corner of the drawing area (see next page):

Click on the **Ellipse** tool.

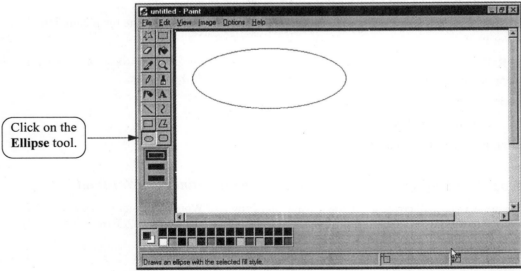

Figure 6 - 15

- o   Use Figure 6 - 15 to guide you.

- o   Click and hold the left mouse button down at the first corner of the ellipse.

- o   Drag to the opposite corner and release the left mouse button.

     You will see the ellipse as you drag the mouse pointer across the screen.

     Next, you will add your name to the picture. You will place your name in the bottom right hand corner of the drawing area, and then move it to the middle of the ellipse.

 8.   At the Tool Box, click on the **Text** tool.

9.   Using the same procedures as in step 7, place a text box in the bottom right corner of the drawing area (Figure 6 - 16).

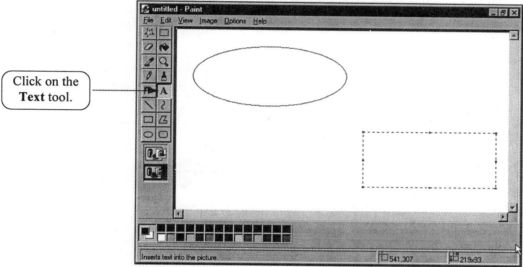

Figure 6 - 16

*The **Fonts** dialog box will appear on the screen (Figure 6 - 17).*

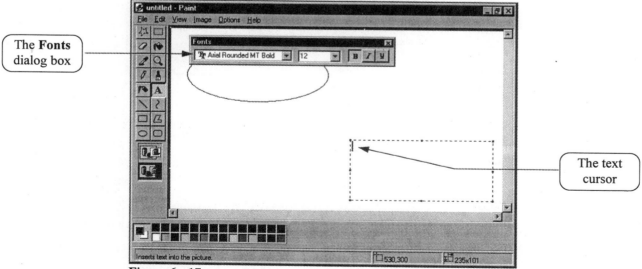

Figure 6 - 17

PROBLEM SOLVER: *If the Fonts dialog box does not appear on the screen, choose VIEW/Text Toolbar.*

10. Make the following changes:

    o   Choose any font style.

    o   Change the text size to **12**.

    o   Click on the **Bold** button.

11. If the text cursor is not blinking in the top left corner of the rectangle, click within the rectangle.

12. Type your name in the text block.

13. Look at the size of your name. If it looks like your name will not fit inside the ellipse which you have drawn, decrease the size of the text in the **Fonts** dialog box.

14. To remove the **Fonts** dialog box, click on a blank spot in the drawing area.

 15. At the Tool Box, click on the **Selection** tool.

16. Drag a box around your name, and then point to the middle of your name.

    The mouse pointer appears as a four-tipped arrow indicating that you will be able to move the text.

17. Drag your name into the middle of the ellipse (Figure 6 - 18).

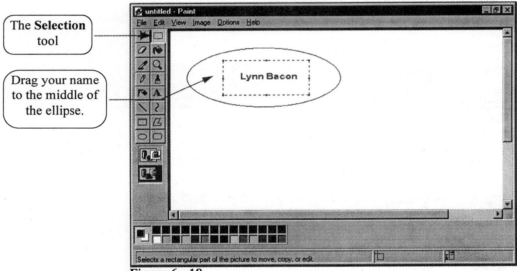

Figure 6 - 18

*You will save the Paint document as **Name Logo** on your data disk. To save space on your disk you will save the Paint document using a 16 Bit Color Bitmap.*

18. Choose **FILE/Save As**.

19. Type **Name Logo** in the **File name** text box.

20. Choose **16 Color Bitmap** from the **Save as type** list box.

21. Choose **3½ Floppy (A:)** (or the location of your data disk) from the **Save in** list box.

22. Click on the **Save** button.

23. Make sure the **Selection** tool is still active, and drag a box around the ellipse (Figure 6 - 19).

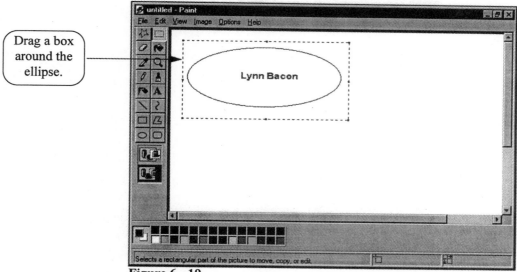

Figure 6 - 19

24. To copy the logo to the Clipboard, click on **EDIT/Copy**.

25. Run *WordPad* and maximize its window.

26. Paste the Paint logo into *WordPad*.

    The name logo will be placed at the top of the page. Handles and a border will appear around the logo (Figure 6 - 20). Unselect the logo by clicking to the right of the border.

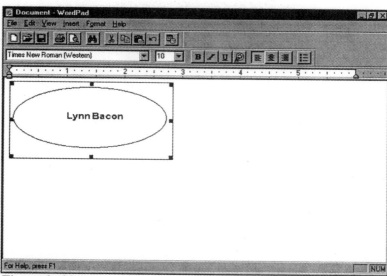

Figure 6 - 20

27. Save the *WordPad* document as **Logo Ellipse Name** on your data disk.

28. Close all the open windows.

    You will return to the Desktop.

Lesson 7 Using the Windows Explorer

Objectives

In this lesson you will learn how to:

- Understand the purpose of the Windows Explorer
- Start the Windows Explorer
- Create a folder
- Move documents

- Copy documents
- Rename documents
- Understand and use the Recycle Bin
- Delete documents and folders
- Expand and collapse folders

MANAGING DOCUMENTS AND FOLDERS IN WINDOWS

Everyone who uses a personal computer becomes, of necessity, a housekeeper. As a housekeeper, what is it that you need to keep in order? Your documents, of course. As you create more and more documents at the computer, being able to organize them in a logical and useful manner is crucial.

Paper documents are saved in file folders—all the documents in a particular folder are placed there because they have something in common that makes them belong together. *Windows 95* uses file folders also. You will create folders (or directories) to save files in. You might create a folder for each course you take during a semester. Then, when you save a paper you have written, you can save it in the folder for its own course.

What other tasks are part of this personal computer housekeeping? Besides creating folders to save your documents in, you will need to know how to copy documents, move documents, rename documents, and delete documents. Suppose a document is kept in one folder, but really belongs in another—move it! Suppose a document could logically belong in two different folders—place a copy of the document in each! Suppose a document's name is just not right—rename it! And, when you have no further use for a document—send it to the Recycle Bin! You will do all these tasks and more as part of what we call document management.

What is the Windows Explorer?

The Windows Explorer is a program that is part of *Windows 95*. It is the area of *Windows 95* designed for what is called document and folder management, although many of the same tasks may be done at the My Computer window. The Windows Explorer replaces the File Manager, which was used in previous versions of *Windows*.

The Windows Explorer displays a comprehensive listing of all the folders and documents on your computer. Its window is divided into two parts. All folders are listed on the left side, or *pane*, of the Explorer window, and the contents of one folder at a time are listed on the right pane. The listing of folders may be expanded or condensed whenever you wish.

What makes the system of storing documents in folders so flexible is that a folder, while containing documents, may also contain sub-folders of its own. For example, you could create a folder called **Spring97**, to contain all your school documents for that semester. Then, you could create four subfolders, one for each of your courses: **Anthropology, British Literature, Accounting, and Journalism**. Finally, *each* of the sub-folders could have sub-folders of its own: **Notes, Papers,** and **Review** for example. During the semester you would be able to save each document you create in a folder with other documents of the same kind.

During Lesson 7, you will learn to understand folder creation and organization, and you will learn to perform the necessary tasks for keeping your computer organized. *Windows 3.1* users will notice that certain vocabulary has changed: what is now called a *folder* used to be called a *directory*, and *documents* used to be called files. These terms are still acceptable, but *Windows 95* uses the new terminology.

REMEMBER: *Read the bulleted list that follows, but do not actually perform the steps until you reach Activity 7.1.*

To start the Windows Explorer:

- Click on the **Start** menu.

- Point to **Programs** and click on **Windows Explorer**.

  Windows Explorer is located at the bottom of the Programs menu.

Activity 7.1: Starting the Windows Explorer

In this activity, you will start the Windows Explorer.

1. Click on the **Start** Menu.

2. Point to **PROGRAMS** and click on **Windows Explorer**.

   Windows Explorer appears on the screen (see Figure 7-1).

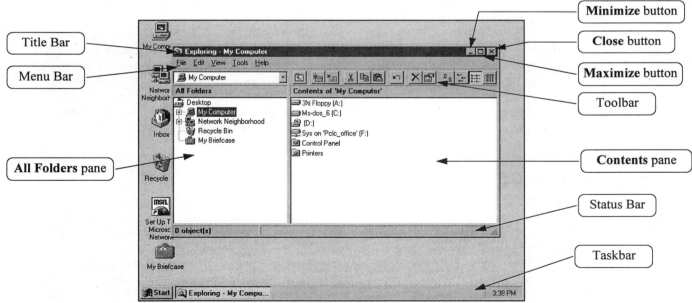

Figure 7 - 1   The Windows 95 Explorer

3. Leave the Windows Explorer open for the next activity.

   If your screen does not match Figure 7-1, do not be concerned. We will work with the screen in the next activity.

Understanding the Windows Explorer Screen

The Windows Explorer contains a Menu Bar, an optional Toolbar and Status Bar, and a two-sided listing. The left side, called the **All Folders** pane, displays folders contained in all drives of the computer, listed hierarchically (by levels). The right side, called the **Contents** pane, displays contents of a single selected folder in the **All Folders** pane. You can change the listing on the **Contents** pane by clicking on a different folder on the **All Folders** pane. The Toolbar has shortcut buttons for many of the housekeeping tasks. You will use the **Cut**, **Copy**, and **Paste** buttons on the Toolbar later in this lesson. The Status Bar contains the number of *objects* (documents, folders, and other files) in the folder that has been selected, and the amount of free disk space on the disk you are looking at.

Activity 7.2: Displaying Elements of the Windows Explorer

In this activity, you will display the Toolbar and Status Bar of the Windows Explorer as well as list folders and documents, so that your screen will match Figure 7-1.

1. The Windows Explorer should be open. If not, repeat Activity 7.1.

2. If the Toolbar is *not* displayed, click on the **View** menu and click on **Toolbar**.

3. If the Status Bar is *not* displayed, click on the **View** menu and click on **Status Bar**.

4. On the left pane of the two-sided list (**All Folders**) scroll to the top and click on the **Desktop** icon.

5. On the left pane of the two-sided list, click on any minus (-) you see in front of a listing. This will change the minus to a plus.

   You have collapsed (condensed) the listing of folders. You will learn more about expanding and collapsing folders in a later activity.

6. If the icons in the right pane (Contents of 'Desktop') are not listed vertically, click on the **View** menu and click on **List**.

   *If you like, you may click on each of the choices in turn (Large Icons, Small Icons, List, and Details), to see how the right pane changes. Your final choice should be: **List**.*

7. Make sure the Explorer window is big enough to display its contents comfortably. If not, enlarge the window.

   Your screen should now closely resemble Figure 7-1, allowing for differences in specific programs that are listed.

8. Leave the Explorer open for the next activity.

In the next group of activities, you will become familiar with the Windows Explorer screen. Then, you will perform the housekeeping tasks already discussed: creating folders, and moving, copying, and renaming documents and folders. You will delete documents and folders using the Recycle Bin.

Creating a Folder

As you begin housekeeping, you will want to create your own folders in which to save your documents. Every new folder you create will be a subfolder of another folder that is at a higher level of the folder hierarchy. The highest level that exists in *Windows 95* is that of the Desktop.

The highest level of folder you can create is a folder at the same level as My Computer, Network Neighborhood, and Recycle Bin.

At the **All Folders** pane, each indentation from the left edge of the pane is considered another level of the hierarchy. The Desktop is the first or highest level, and it is listed at the leftmost position within the pane. My Computer, Network Neighborhood, and Recycle Bin are indented one level, meaning that each is a sub-folder of the Desktop. Another analogy often used with this hierarchy is 'parent and child'. The parent level is the level above a folder and the child level is the level below a folder. In this example, the Desktop would be the parent of My Computer, Network Neighborhood, and Recycle Bin. They would all be considered children of the Desktop.

To create a folder:

- Click on the parent (the folder that will appear one level above the new folder).

- At the Menu Bar, click on **FILE/New**.

  A submenu appears.

- Select **Folder** from the submenu.

  *A **folder** icon appears at the end of the **Contents** pane list at the right side of the screen. The name of the folder is **New Folder** and the text is highlighted so that when you start typing, the current text will be replaced.*

- Type the name of the new folder.

  The text you type replaces the current text.

- Press **ENTER**.

  NOTE: *Folders appear in alphabetical order at the top of the Contents list. However, the screen will not show the alphabetized location of the folder automatically. You can select **VIEW/Refresh** to update the screen display.*

Activity 7.3: Checking the Data Disk

In this activity, you will make sure you have the documents you need to proceed with this lesson.

1. The Windows Explorer should be open. If not, repeat Activities 7.1 and 7.2.

2. Insert your data disk into the appropriate disk drive.

3. If there is a plus in front of the folder for **My Computer** click on the plus. If there is a minus showing, do nothing.

   You should see the floppy drive that contains your data disk listed. It will be listed one indentation to the right of the My Computer icon.

4. Maximize the Explorer.

5. At the Menu Bar, click on **VIEW/List**.

6. Click on **VIEW/Arrange Icons/By Name**.

7. In the **All Folders** pane, click on the floppy drive containing your data disk (see Figure 7-2).

   You will see a complete list of all the documents you have saved as you completed each activity and Independent Project in Lessons 1 through 6. You will need to have these documents available for the activities in Lesson 7.

8. Compare the documents on your screen with those in Figure 7-2.

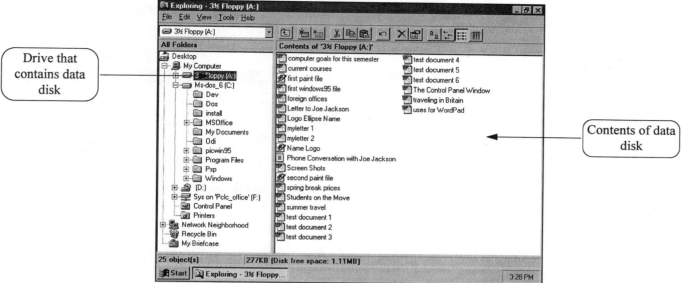

Figure 7 - 2

9. If you have all these documents, proceed directly to Activity 7.4. If you do *not* have all these documents, you will create substitute documents as follows:

   o Minimize the Explorer.

   o Run *WordPad*.

   o Re-read Lesson 2, Activity 2.7, Steps 10-18.

   o Using the procedure described, create *fifteen* substitute documents, saving each on your data disk. Name them **substitute 1**, **substitute 2**, etc.

   o After the substitute documents have been saved, close WordPad and Restore the Explorer.

   o As you complete the activities in Lesson 7, use the designated documents whenever possible. If you do not have a document, use the substitute document that will be suggested instead.

10. Leave the Explorer open and maximized for the next activity.

Activity 7.4: Creating a Folder

In this activity, you will create a new folder on your data disk. In Activity 7.5, you will copy and move documents to this folder.

1. The Windows Explorer should be open and maximized. Make sure **VIEW/List** has been chosen.

2. If necessary, insert your data disk into the appropriate disk drive.

3. As in Figure 7-2, click on the listing for the drive containing your data disk.

4. Look at the **Contents** pane (right side) to see the list of documents that have been saved on your data disk.

5. At the Menu Bar, click on **FILE/New**.

6. Click on **Folder**.

*A new folder icon appears in the **Contents** pane with the label, **New Folder**, highlighted so that when you begin typing, the text will be replaced.*

7.   Type: **Current Projects** and press **ENTER** (see Figure 7-3).

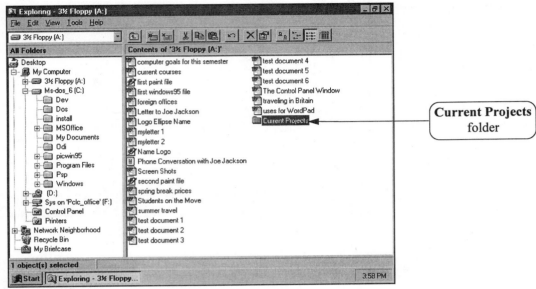

Figure 7 - 3

*You will see the new folder. Folders should be listed before documents on the **Contents** pane. You will refresh the screen so that you can see the new folder at the top of the list.*

8.   Click on **VIEW/Refresh**.

*The **Current Projects** folder is displayed at the top of the Contents list.*

9.   To see the **Current Projects** listed on the **All Folders** pane, click on the plus (+) that has just appeared in front of the listing for the drive containing your data disk.

Your new folder, Current Projects, will be displayed below the drive listing, indented one level to show that it is a sub-folder of the floppy drive. Your screen should resemble Figure 7-4.

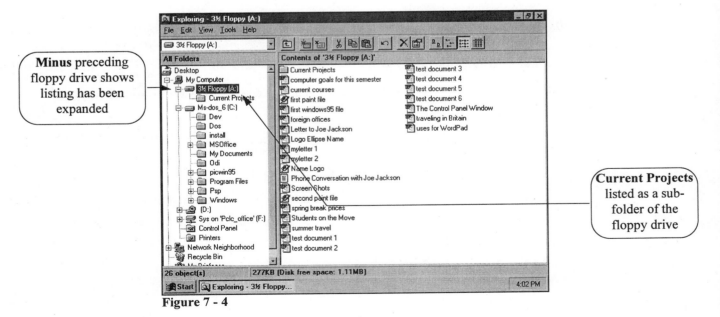

Figure 7 - 4

10. To create another folder, leave the drive containing your data disk selected.

11. At the Menu Bar, click on **FILE/New**.

12. Click on **Folder**.

13. Type: **Completed Projects**

14. Press **ENTER**.

15. At the Menu Bar, click on **VIEW/Refresh**.

You have now created another folder. Notice that the folders and documents are arranged in two separately alphabetized sets of listings. Your screen should resemble Figure 7-5.

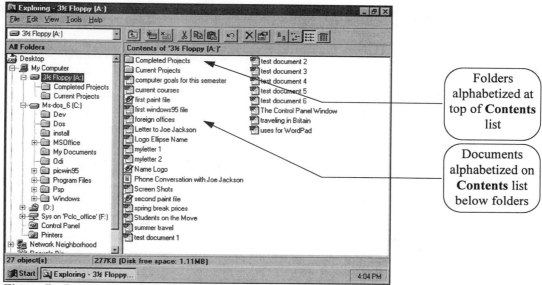

Figure 7 - 5

16. Leave the Windows Explorer open for the next activity.

Moving and Copying Documents

Being able to copy or move a document from one folder to another is a necessary part of being successfully organized at the computer. There are several ways to move and copy documents in *Windows 95*. You can use the Menu Bar by clicking on **EDIT/Cut** or **EDIT/Copy** and **EDIT/Paste**, or you can use the Toolbar as a shortcut by clicking on the **Cut** or **Copy** button and the **Paste** button. You can also move or copy single documents or groups of documents from one folder to another by clicking on the document icon(s) and dragging the icon (s) to a different folder. This method is called **Drag and Drop**.

To Copy or Move a document from one folder to another: (Toolbar method)

• Click on the folder containing the document in the **All Folders** pane.

• Select the document you wish to copy or move from the **Contents** pane.

*To select a single document, click on the document name. To select multiple contiguous (or adjacent) documents, click on the first document, press the **SHIFT** key down, and then click on the last document in the list. To select multiple non-contiguous (or non-adjacent) files, click on a filename, press the **CTRL** key down, and click on the next document name. Continue this process, keeping the **CTRL** key pressed down until all the documents you wish to select are selected.*

- Click on the **Cut** button if you wish to move the document or click on the **Copy** button if you wish to copy the document.

- Click on the folder in the **All Folders** pane to which you want to move the selected document(s).

- Click on the **Paste** button .

The selected document(s) will be moved or copied to the new folder.

Activity 7.5: *Moving and Copying Documents*

In this activity, you will copy and move documents to the **Current Projects** and **Completed Projects** folders which you created in Activity 7.4.

1. Make sure that the Windows Explorer is open and maximized, with the drive containing your data disk selected in the **All Folders** pane.

2. If necessary, click on the plus sign to the left of the drive icon containing your disk in the **All Folders** pane so that the folders for **Current Projects** and **Completed Projects** folders appear below the drive.

3. In the **Contents** pane, click on the listing for **first windows95 file**. If you do not have this document you may use **substitute 1** (created in Activity 7.3) instead.

4. Hold down the **CONTROL** key (**CTRL**) and click on the listing for **first paint file**. If you do not have this document you may use **substitute 2** (created in Activity 7.3) instead.

   *Now, two documents have been selected. Holding down the **CONTROL** key lets you select as many documents as you like, regardless of where they appear on the list.*

5. At the Toolbar, click on the **Cut** button. If the Toolbar is not visible, click on **VIEW/Toolbar**.

6. At the **All Folders** pane, click on the **Completed Projects** folder.

7. At the Toolbar, click on the **Paste** button.

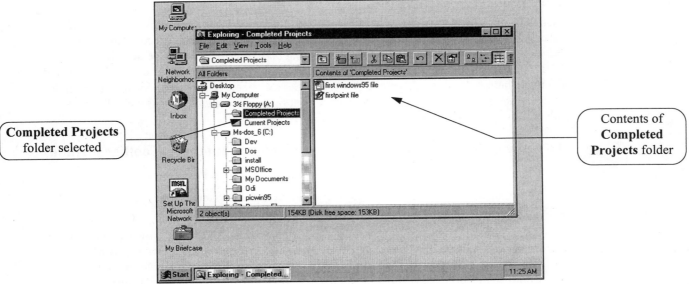

Completed Projects folder selected

Contents of **Completed Projects** folder

Figure 7 - 6

You will see an image of the documents moving from one folder to another. The documents will appear on the **Contents** *pane (see Figure 7-6).*

8. In the **All Folders** pane, click on the listing for the floppy drive that contains your data disk.

9. In the **Contents** pane, click on the document called **test document 3**. If you do not have this document you may use **substitute 3** (created in Activity 7.3) instead.

10. While holding down the **SHIFT** key, click on **test document 5**. If you do not have this document you may use **substitute 5** (created in Activity 7.3) instead.

    Holding down the **SHIFT** *key allows you to select a group of documents that are contiguous (adjacent on the list of documents). Both documents you clicked on, and all the documents between them have been selected.*

11. At the Toolbar, click on the **Cut** button.

12. At the **All Folders** pane, click on the **completed projects** folder.

13. Click on the **Paste** button.

    Again, you will see an image of the documents moving from one folder to another as they are moved from their current folder to the **Completed Projects** *folder. The documents will appear on the* **Contents** *pane (see Figure 7-7).*

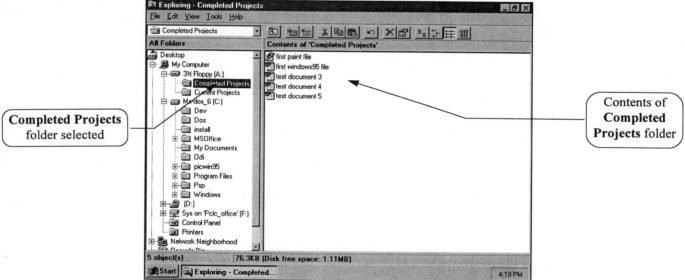

Completed Projects folder selected

Contents of **Completed Projects** folder

Figure 7 - 7

14. In the **All Folders** pane, click on the listing for the floppy drive containing your data disk.

15. At the **Contents** pane, click on the document called **traveling in Britain**. If you do not have this document you may use **substitute 6** (created in Activity 7.3) instead.

16. At the Toolbar, click on the **Copy** button.

17. At the **All Folders** pane, click on the **Current Projects** folder.

18. At the Toolbar, click on the **Paste** button. Your screen should resemble Figure 7-8.

19. At the **All Folders** pane, click on the listing for the floppy drive containing your data disk.

20. Leave the Windows Explorer open for the next activity.

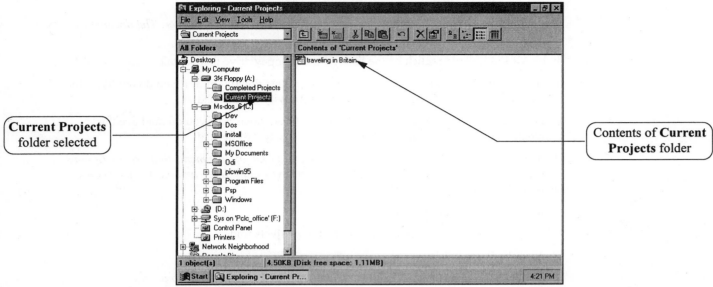

Current Projects folder selected

Contents of **Current Projects** folder

Figure 7 - 8

Renaming Documents

Renaming a document is another useful housekeeping task. The flexibility you gain when you are able to change the name of a document makes it possible to continue to refine your file organization over time without being hampered by inappropriate document names.

To rename a document:

- Click on the document you wish to rename in the **Contents** pane.
- Click on **FILE/Rename**.

  The text for the document becomes highlighted and surrounded with a text block.

- Type the new document name.

  The new text replaces the old.

- Press **ENTER**.

Activity 7.6: Renaming a Document

In this activity you will select a WordPad document created in Lesson 2 and rename it.

1. At the **All Folders** pane of the Windows Explorer, click on the **Completed Projects** folder.

   The contents of the folder appear in the Contents pane.

2. Click on the **test document 5** document (or **substitute 5**).

3. At the Menu Bar, click on **FILE/Rename**.

   The document name is highlighted and surrounded with a frame (see Figure 7-9).

4. Type: **term paper outline** and press **ENTER**.

   The old text is replaced.

5. At the Menu Bar, click on **VIEW/Refresh**.

   Notice how the renamed document is alphabetized (see Figure 7-10).

6. Leave the Windows Explorer open for the next activity.

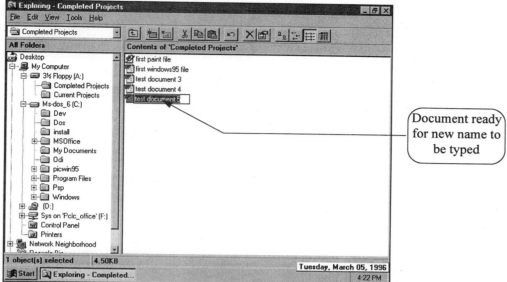

Figure 7 - 9

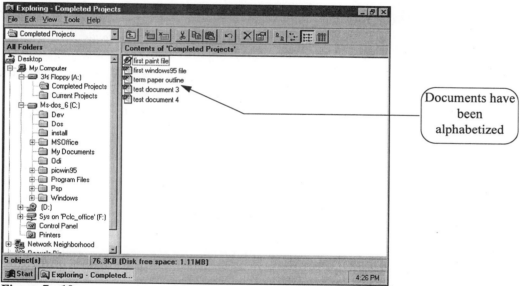

Figure 7 - 10

DELETING DOCUMENTS AND FOLDERS

When you have no further need for a document or folder, you can delete it. Deleting unwanted documents and folders keeps your disks better organized and makes space available for new files. Documents and folders saved on floppy disks may be deleted by pressing the **DELETE** key. Documents saved on the hard disk or on a network may be sent to the Recycle Bin.

The Recycle Bin

When documents and folders are deleted from the hard drive or from a network drive, they may be placed in the Recycle Bin. The Recycle Bin icon is found on the Desktop. You will be able to tell if there are documents in the Recycle Bin just by looking at it! Minimize the Explorer and look at your Recycle Bin now and notice if it is empty or full.

The advantage of sending a document to the Recycle Bin is that documents sent there are not immediately deleted. Instead, the documents remain in the Recycle Bin until they are either restored (brought back into a window), or emptied out of the Recycle Bin (deleted). Thus, the Recycle Bin acts as a holding cell for the documents and folders. When you know for sure that you want the contents of the Recycle Bin deleted, you can empty it. You may empty all the documents from the bin or just selected ones. The Recycle Bin gives you a last level of safety, so that you do not delete documents by mistake.

Remember that you cannot send documents saved on a floppy disk to the Recycle Bin. Because the disk containing those documents is not a permanent part of your computer system, the Recycle Bin will not accept them (see Caution below).

CAUTION: *Only documents and folders deleted from the hard drive (C:) or from a network drive will be placed in the Recycle Bin. If you delete documents or folders from your data diskette, they are not deposited into the Recycle Bin. BEWARE! They are automatically deleted!*

NOTE: *To create space on the hard drive (C:), you can empty the Recycle Bin.*

To send a document to the Recycle Bin:

- In any window that lists documents, select the document(s) you wish to delete.

  NOTE: *The process for selecting single, multiple contiguous, and multiple non-contiguous documents is the same as described in the copying and moving documents section.*

- At the Windows Explorer, click on the **Delete** button on the Toolbar, or at any time, press the **DELETE** key.

  *The **Confirm File Delete** dialog box appears on the screen. Its purpose is to confirm that you want to delete the selected file(s) and in so doing, remove the files to the Recycle Bin.*

- Click on **Yes**.

  The file is deposited in the Recycle Bin.

To send a folder to the Recycle Bin:

- Select the folder you wish to delete.

  CAUTION: *When you delete a folder, you also delete the contents of the folder. Make sure before deleting a folder that you also want to delete **ALL** of the documents in the folder!*

- At the Windows Explorer, click on the **Delete** button on the Toolbar, or at any time, press the **DELETE** key.

  *The **Confirm Folder Delete** dialog box appears on the screen. Its purpose is to confirm that you want to delete the selected folder and its contents and in so doing, remove the folder and its contents to the Recycle Bin.*

- Click on **Yes**.

  The folder and its contents are sent to the Recycle Bin.

Using the Recycle Bin

Once the Recycle Bin is no longer empty, you will want to look inside. One reason for doing so is to restore documents you deleted by accident. Another reason is to free up disk space on the hard drive by emptying the Recycle Bin.

To open the Recycle Bin:

- Point to the Recycle Bin on the Desktop and double-click the left mouse button.

  The Recycle Bin window appears on the screen with a list of the documents that have been deposited in it. Along with the name of the document, the original location of the document and the date and time the document was deleted is listed.

To restore a document that has been deleted:

- Click on the document you wish to restore in the Recycle Bin window.
- At the Menu Bar, click on **FILE/Restore**.

To empty the Recycle Bin:

- At the Recycle Bin Menu Bar, click on **FILE/Empty Recycle Bin**.

Activity 7.7: Looking at the Recycle Bin

In this activity, you will not actually send documents to the Recycle Bin or empty the Recycle Bin because of the risk of deleting an important document by mistake. We will open the Recycle Bin and examine its window.

1. Close the Windows Explorer.

2. Close any other open windows.

3. Examine the icon for the Recycle Bin on the Desktop.

   If the Bin icon contains paper, there are documents inside. If it is empty, there is nothing inside.

4. Double-click on the icon to open the Recycle Bin (see Figure 7-11).

   If there are no documents in your Recycle Bin the main area of the window will be empty. If other elements of the window are not displayed, follow Steps 5-8.

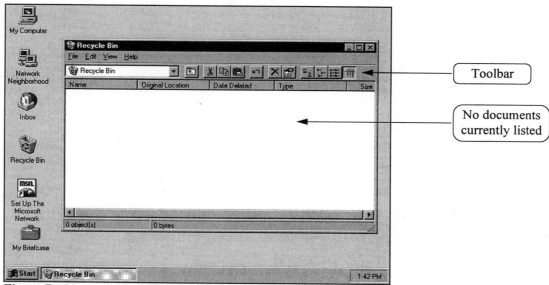

Figure 7 - 11   **The Recycle Bin when it is Empty**

5. If necessary, display the toolbar by clicking on **VIEW/Toolbar**.

6. If necessary, display the Status Bar by clicking on **VIEW/Status Bar**.

7. Make sure the window is big enough to see the contents.

8. If necessary, display the details for files that are listed by clicking on **VIEW/Details**.

9. If your Recycle Bin is *not* empty, examine the listing of items in it.

   Each listing contains the name of the item, the location from which it was sent to the Recycle Bin, the date and time it was sent and the type of document.

10. Click on the **File** menu and notice the **Empty Recycle Bin** command. **Do not click the command**.

11. Close the **File** menu.

12. Close the Recycle Bin window.

13. Leave *Windows 95* running.

Activity 7.8: Deleting a document from a floppy disk

In this activity, you will delete a document you saved on your data disk. The document will not go to the Recycle Bin, but will be deleted.

1. Open the Windows Explorer and maximize it.

2. On the **All Folders** pane, click on the drive containing your data disk.

3. On the Contents list, click on **current courses**. If you do not have this document you may use **substitute 7** (created in Activity 7.3) instead.

4. Press the **DELETE** key.

5. You will see a **Confirm File Delete** box asking you if you are sure you want to delete the document (see Figure 7-12).

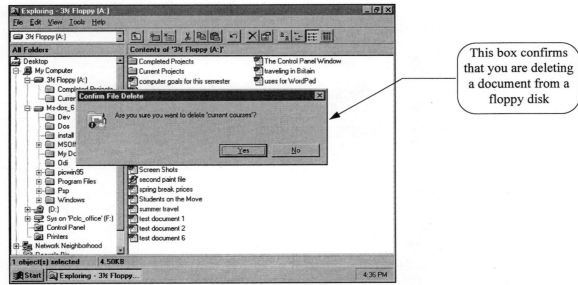

Figure 7 - 12

6. Answer **Yes**.

   The document will be deleted.

7. Leave the Windows Explorer open for the next activity.

EXPANDING AND COLLAPSING FOLDERS

As you learned earlier in this lesson, the folders in the **All Folder** pane are displayed in a hierarchical fashion. In addition, folders may be displayed or hidden from the list. Displaying and hiding folders is called *expanding* and *collapsing* the list.

As you have seen, some of the folders in the **All Folders** pane are preceded by a plus or minus. The minus sign indicates that the folder contains sub-folders that are currently displayed. Removing the display of the sub-folders is called collapsing.

The plus sign indicates that the folder contains sub-folders that are currently hidden. Expanding a folder means displaying its sub-folders.

To expand a folder so that its sub-folders are displayed:

- Click on the plus sign to the left of the folder.

All sub-folders will appear.

To collapse a folder so that its sub-folders are hidden:

- Click on the minus sign to the left of the folder.

The folder's sub-folders will be hidden

Activity 7.9: Expanding and Collapsing Folders

In this activity, you will expand and collapse folders in the **All Folders** pane.

1. Open the Windows Explorer and maximize, if necessary.

2. In the **All Folders** pane, click on **My Computer** and examine the plusses and minuses.

   An expanded drive or directory will have a minus sign in the box to the left of the icon. A collapsed folder will have a plus sign in the box to the left of the icon (see Figure 7-13).

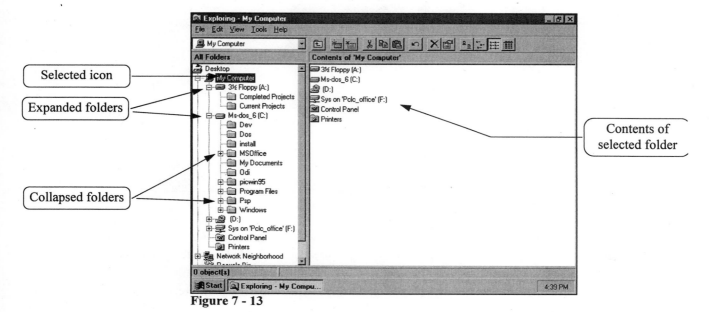

Figure 7 - 13

3. Click on any minus signs showing so that the **All Folders** pane is completely collapsed (see Figure 7-14).

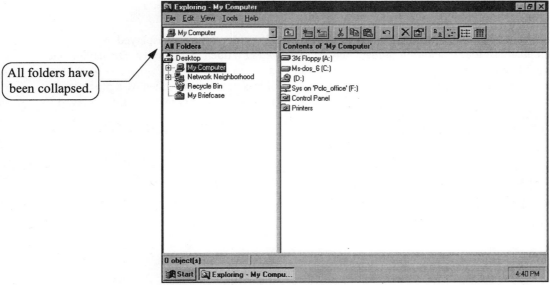

All folders have been collapsed.

Figure 7 - 14

4. Click on the plus sign next to **My Computer**.

   *The **All Folders** pane expands to show the drives on your computer as well as the Control Panel and Printers folders (Figure 7-15).*

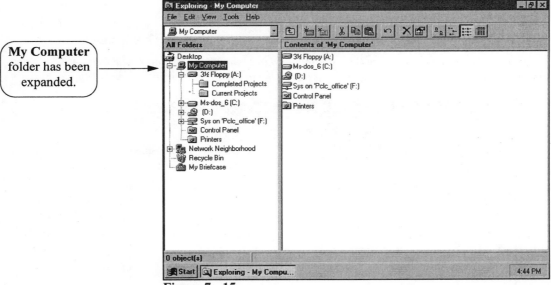

My Computer folder has been expanded.

Figure 7 - 15

PROBLEM SOLVER: *If your screen does not resemble Figure 7-15, click on any minus signs that appear other than the ones that precede the **My Computer** icon and the floppy drive icon.*

5. Click on the plus sign next to the **C:** drive. After you click your screen should resemble Figure 7-16.

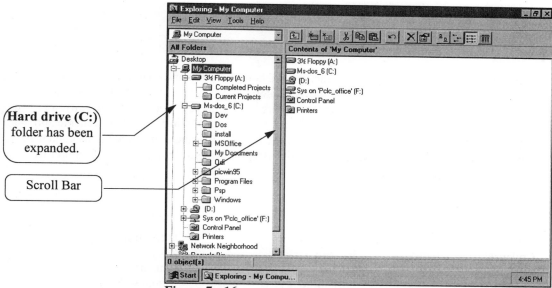

Hard drive (C:)
folder has been
expanded.

Scroll Bar

Figure 7 - 16

*The **All Folders** pane expands to show the folders available on the C: drive. It will not be exact because you will have different software installed on your computer.*

6. Use the scroll bar (Figure 7-16) next to the **All Folders** pane to scroll down to the **Windows** folder.

7. Click on the plus sign next to the **Windows** folder.

*There are many sub-folders contained in the **Windows** folder.*

8. Scroll down until you see the **Start Menu** folder.

9. Click on the plus sign next to the **Start Menu** folder.

*The **Programs** folder appears below the **Start Menu** folder. Notice that the folder has a slightly different icon (Figure 7-17). If **Programs** has not been expanded, you will not see the sub-folders listed beneath it. You may adjust your screen if you wish.*

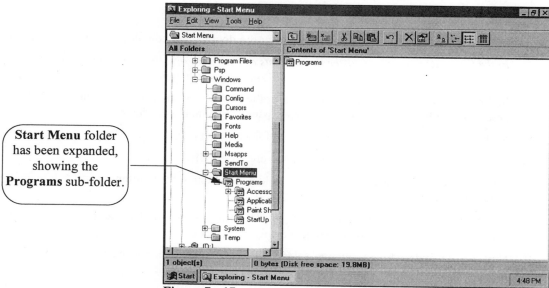

Start Menu folder
has been expanded,
showing the
Programs sub-folder.

Figure 7 - 17

10. Close the Windows Explorer.

SUMMARY

In this lesson, you learned about and practiced the housekeeping tasks necessary for everyone who uses a personal computer using the Windows Explorer. You learned to run the Explorer and understand its screen. You learned to create folders for saving your documents logically, and you learned to move and copy your documents from one folder to another, as well as rename and delete your documents. You practiced opening the Recycle Bin and understanding its contents. Finally, you learned to control the listing of folders in the All Folders pane of the Explorer by expanding and collapsing their display.

KEY TERMS

All Folders pane	Drag and Drop	Properties
Collapse	Expand	Recycle Bin
Contents pane	Folder	Rename
Copy	Formatting a Disk	Running Programs
Cut	Large Icons	Small Icons
Delete	List	Toolbar
Details	Pane	VIEW/Refresh
Document	Paste	Windows Explorer

INDEPENDENT PROJECTS

The independent projects will reinforce the housekeeping tasks you learned in this lesson: creating folders and sub-folders; copying, moving, and renaming, and deleting documents; and expanding and collapsing folders in the **All Folders** pane.

Independent Project 7.1: Creating Folders and Sub-Folders

In this project, you will create additional folders and sub-folders on your data disk.

1. Turn on your computer and insert your data disk in the floppy drive.

2. Run the Windows Explorer.

3. In the **All Folders** pane, click on the folder for the floppy drive containing your data disk.

   In the Contents pane, you will see the contents of your data disk listed, including the two folders you created in Lesson 7, Completed Projects and Current Projects.

4. In the **All Folders** pane, expand the listing of the floppy drive by clicking on the plus that precedes it. If the listing has already been expanded, you may skip this step.

5. With the floppy drive selected, create a new folder on your data disk.

6. Type the name for the folder: **Drawings** and press **ENTER**.

7. Click on **VIEW/Refresh** to bring the new folder to the top of the **Contents** pane, following the other folders.

8. In the **All Folders** pane, click on the new folder, **Drawings**, and notice that the **Contents** pane is empty (because there are no documents in the folder).

9. Create a sub-folder of the **Drawings** folder, following the instructions in Step 5.

10. Type the name for the folder: **Logos** and press **ENTER**.

11. In the **All Folders** pane, select the **Completed Projects** folder.

12. Create a sub-folder within **Completed Projects** called **Books**.

13. Refresh the screen.

14. In the **All Folders** pane, expand the listings for the **Completed Projects** and **Drawings** folders. Your listing of the floppy drive in the **All Folders** pane should resemble Figure 7-18.

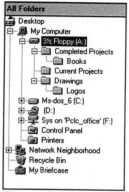

All Folders
```
Desktop
My Computer
    3½ Floppy (A:)
        Completed Projects
            Books
        Current Projects
        Drawings
            Logos
    Ms-dos_6 (C:)
    (D:)
    Sys on 'Pclc_office' (F:)
    Control Panel
    Printers
Network Neighborhood
Recycle Bin
My Briefcase
```

Figure 7-18

15. Press **PRINTSCREEN** to send the screen image to the Clipboard.

16. Minimize the Explorer.

17. Run WordPad, type your name and date, and paste the Clipboard contents.

18. Press **CTRL+HOME** to reach the top of the WordPad document.

19. Print the document.

20. Close WordPad without saving the document.

21. Close the Explorer.

Independent Project 7.2: Moving and Copying Documents

In this project, you will move and copy documents to the new folders you created in the previous project. You will use the *right mouse button* for moving and copying the documents. This is a challenging project.

1. Turn on your computer, insert your data disk, and run the *Windows 95* Explorer.

2. In the **All Folders** pane, click on the folder for the drive containing your data disk.

3. In the **Contents** pane, you will see three folders, **Completed Projects**, **Current Projects**, and **Drawings** listed, and a number of documents.

4. In the **All Folders** pane, make sure all folders on the drive containing your data disk have been expanded so that their sub-folders are displayed (see Figure 7-18).

5. In the **Contents** pane, click on **second paint file**. If you do not have this file available, you may use **substitute 8** instead.

6. To move the document to the **Drawings** folder using the Drag and Drop method, press the *right mouse button* while pointing to the document, and drag it on top of the **Drawings** folder. You may drag it onto the **Drawings** folder in the **All Folders** pane, *or* the **Drawings** folder in the **Contents** pane.

7. Release the mouse button and click on **Move here**.

*The document will be moved to the **Drawings** folder.*

8. To check that the document has been moved, click on the **Drawings** folder on the **All Folders** pane, and look in the **Contents** pane.

9. In the **All Folders** pane, click on the folder called **Completed Projects**.

10. In the **Contents** pane, click on **first paint file**. You may have **substitute 2** listed instead.

11. To move the document to the **Drawings** folder, using the *right mouse button*, drag the document to the **All Folders** pane and position it on the **Drawings** folder.

12. Release the mouse button and click on **Move here**.

*The document will be moved to the **Drawings** folder.*

13. Making sure that **Completed Projects** is still selected in the **All Folders** pane, In the **Contents** pane, click on **test document 3**, hold down the **SHIFT** key, and click on **test document 4**. You may have **substitute 3** and **substitute 4** on your list instead.

14. To copy the documents to the **Books** folder (a sub-folder of **Completed Projects** created in Independent Project 7.1), using the *right mouse button*, drag the documents to the **All Folders** pane and position the mouse pointer on top of the **Books** folder.

If you do not have this folder, create it now and then return to Step 13.

15. Release the mouse button and click on **Copy here**.

The documents will be copied.

16. In the **All Folders** pane, click on the folder for the floppy drive containing your data disk.

17. In the **Contents** pane, click on **Name Logo**, a document you created in Lesson 6. If you do not have this document, use **substitute 9** instead.

18. Using the *right mouse button*, drag and drop the document to the **Logos** folder (**Logos** is a sub-folder of **Drawings**).

*If you do not have the **Logos** folder, create it now and return to Step 17.*

19. Release the mouse and click on **Move here**.

20. In the **All Folders** pane, click on the **Books** folder so that its contents are displayed on the **Contents** pane.

21. Press **PRINTSCREEN** to copy the screen image to the Clipboard.

22. Open WordPad and paste the contents of the Clipboard.

23. Unselect the image you just pasted so that no handles show around its edges.

24. Return to the Explorer.

25. In the **All Folders** pane, click on the **Drawings** folder.

26. Press **PRINTSCREEN.**

27. Return to WordPad and press **CTRL+END** to reach the end of the document.

28. Paste the new Clipboard contents into WordPad.

29. Press **CTRL+END** again, and type your name and date at the end of the document.

30. Print the WordPad document, which consists of two screen images, your name, and date.

31. Close WordPad without saving.

32. Close the Explorer.

Independent Project 7.3: Renaming and Deleting Documents

In this project, you will rename and delete documents from your data disk. This is a challenging project.

1. Turn on your computer and insert your data disk into the appropriate drive.

2. Run the Windows 95 Explorer.

3. In the **All Folders** pane, click on the folder for the floppy drive containing your data disk.

4. In the **Contents** pane, click on **summer travel**. If you do not have this file you may use **substitute 10** instead.

5. Rename the document: **request for summer info**.

6. Rename **traveling in britain** so that the name reads: **reply to summer inquiry**. If you do not have the document, you may use **substitute 11** instead.

7. In the **All Folders** pane, expand the listing for the floppy drive so that all folders on your data disk are displayed.

8. In the **All Folders** pane, click on the **Books** folder.

9. In the **Contents** pane, delete **test document 3** (or **substitute 3**).

10. Delete **test document 4** (or **substitute 4**) also.

11. In the **All Folders** pane, click on the folder called **Completed Projects**.

12. Rename the document **term paper outline** with the name: **Hamlet paper outline**. If you do not have the document, you may rename **substitute 5** instead.

13. In the **All Folders** pane, click on the **logos** folder.

14. Rename **Name Logo** so that the name reads: **Name inside Ellipse Logo**. If you do not have the document, you may rename **substitute 9** instead.

15. With the renamed document showing in the **Contents** pane, press **PRINTSCREEN** once more and add the contents of the Clipboard to a WordPad document.

16. Unselect the pasted image in WordPad, and add your name to the end of the document.

17. Print the WordPad document and close WordPad without saving.

18. Close the *Windows 95* Explorer.

Lesson

8 Customizing Windows 95 with Shortcuts

Objectives

In this lesson you will learn how to:

- Create shortcuts
- Add a shortcut for a program to the Start menu
- Add a shortcut for a program to the Desktop

- Create a shortcut for a document
- Remove shortcuts from the Start menu and Desktop
- Use the **Find** feature to locate a file

WHAT ARE SHORTCUTS?

A shortcut is an icon you create to represent a program or a document. After you create it you then position it in a convenient place so it is easily at hand when you are working. The shortcut icon will work exactly as the original icon does.

For instance, suppose you frequently use the **Notepad** to jot down ideas or phone numbers as you work or speak on the phone. To open the **Notepad**, you have to begin at the **Start** button and move the mouse several columns over and then down. You may decide instead to create a shortcut for the **Notepad** and place it right on the Start menu.

Perhaps you have an *Excel* document that you use daily to chart the opening and closing prices of your investments. You begin by opening *Excel*, and then you open that document. Instead, you may create a shortcut icon for the document and place the shortcut directly on the Desktop. When you click on the icon, *Excel* and the document will open simultaneously.

The general idea is that no two people use the computer in exactly the same way. Customizing *Windows 95* to your own needs and preferences will result in greater efficiency and productivity for you. We began this process in Lesson 3 as you learned to control the settings of *Windows 95* at the Control Panel. We continue now in Lesson 8 by learning to create and use shortcuts.

CREATING A PROGRAM SHORTCUT

There are several ways of creating shortcuts in *Windows 95*; we will learn the simplest method.

REMEMBER: *Read the bulleted list that follows, but do not actually perform the steps until you reach Activity 8.1.*

To create a shortcut for a program:

- Double-click on the **My Computer** icon on the Desktop.
- From the My Computer window, open the window that contains the icon and listing for the program.

  *If you do not know where to find the icon, use the **Find** feature, described later in the lesson.*

- In that window, click on the icon for the program you are interested in.
- Drag the icon to the Start menu, the Desktop or wherever you wish the shortcut to be located.

  *For example, you may drag it to the **Start** button or you may place it on the Desktop. This will copy, not move the icon from its current window. The copied icon will be called: **Shortcut to ...***

- Optional: If you want to rename the shortcut, click on its name, type the new name for the shortcut, and press **ENTER**.

Activity 8.1: Creating a Shortcut icon for the Notepad

In this activity you will create a shortcut icon for the **Notepad** program. You will place the shortcut icon on the Start menu.

1. Open *Windows 95* if it is not already open.
2. Double-click on the **My Computer** icon on the desktop.
3. Double-click on the icon for the **hard drive** (drive **C:**) of your computer.

   *Clicking on drive **C:** opens a window which displays its sub-folders.*

   PROBLEM SOLVER: *If you are working in a computer lab, you may not be allowed to choose this drive. Another possibility is that the file you are looking for may be on a different drive. If so, ask your instructor or lab assistant for help.*

4. Scroll the **hard drive** window and double-click on the folder called **Windows**.

   *Double-clicking on **Windows** opens a window which contains a folder for each program stored in **Windows**.*

5. Scroll the **Windows** window horizontally or vertically, depending on how your window looks, and click on the icon for the file called **Notepad** (see Figure 8-1).

   As you scroll the window, remember that the folders are listed first, followed by the individual program files, arranged in alphabetical order.

   PROBLEM SOLVER: *If the files are not listed in alphabetical order, click on the **View** menu and then point to **Arrange Icons, By Name**. Then, look for the **Notepad** file.*

My Computer window

Hard drive (C:) window

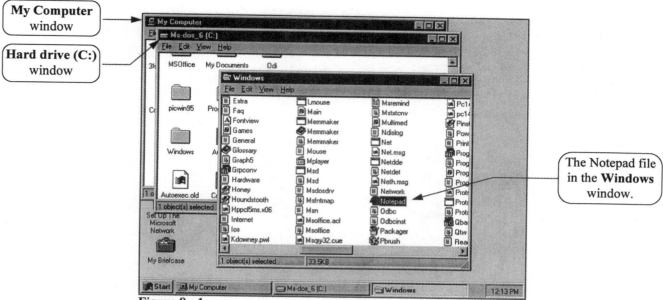

The Notepad file in the **Windows** window.

Figure 8 - 1

6.   Using the left mouse button, drag the **Notepad** icon down to the Taskbar, position it on top of the **Start** button, and release the mouse button (see Figure 8-2).

Positioning the icon on the **Start** button.

Figure 8 - 2

This copies the Notepad icon to the Start menu. As you drag the icon onto the Desktop, notice the Curved arrow beneath the icon. This means the copied icon is a shortcut, not the original Notepad icon.

7.   Click on the **Start** button to make sure that the Notepad shortcut is listed there. It will be at or near the top of the list (see Figure 8-3).

If the icon is not there, try Step 6 again.

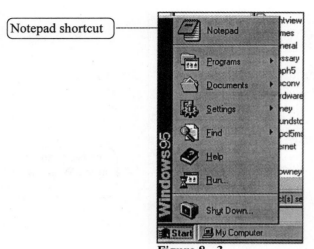

Notepad shortcut

Figure 8 - 3

8. Click on the **Start** button again to close the Start menu.

9. Close all open windows.

10. To test the shortcut, click on the Start button and click on the **Notepad** shortcut.

    The Notepad will run.

11. Close the Notepad.

12. Leave *Windows 95* open for the next activity.

Activity 8.2: Placing a Shortcut Icon on the Desktop

In this activity we will create a shortcut icon for the **WordPad** program and place it on the Desktop. If you cannot locate the WordPad file, ask your instructor for help.

1. Open *Windows 95*, if it is not already running.

2. Double-click on the **My Computer** icon on the Desktop.

3. In the **My Computer** window, double-click on the icon for the hard disk (drive **C:**) of your computer.

4. In the **hard disk (C:)**window, double-click on the folder called **Program Files**.

5. In the **Program Files** window, double-click on the folder called **Accessories**.

6. In the **Accessories** window, click on **WordPad** to select it (see Figure 8-4). Do **not** double-click or the program will run.

7. Using the left mouse button, drag the WordPad icon onto any part of the Desktop you can see. The icon will be named: **Shortcut to WordPad.**

 PROBLEM SOLVER: *If any windows have been maximized you will not be able to see the Desktop. Click the Restore button on any window that has been maximized.*

8. Close all the open windows so that you can see the new icon (see Figure 8-5). If you want to move it, drag it to a different part of the Desktop.

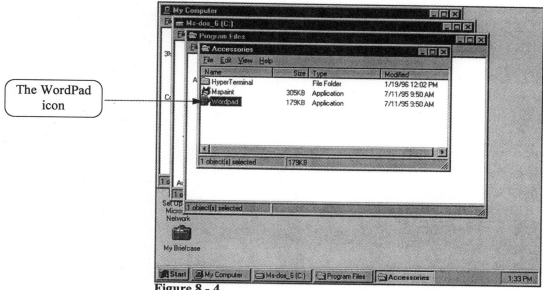

Figure 8 - 4

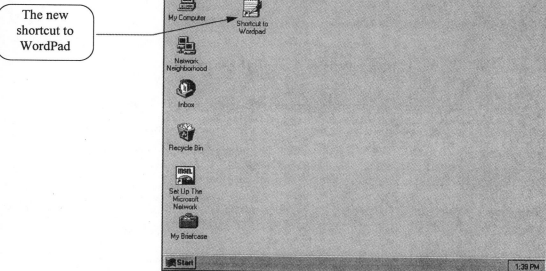

Figure 8 - 5

9. To rename the icon, click lightly on its name (not on the icon) so that the name has a frame around it (see Figure 8-6).

Figure 8 - 6

10. Type the new name: **WordPad** and press **ENTER**.

*Even though **Shortcut** is no longer part of its name, you will know the icon is a shortcut because of the curved arrow on the bottom.*

11. To test the shortcut, double-click on it to run *WordPad*.

12. Close *WordPad*.

13. Leave *Windows 95* open for the next activity.

Deleting Shortcuts

The procedure for deleting a shortcut from the Start menu is different from the procedure for deleting a shortcut from the Desktop.

To delete a shortcut from the Start menu:

- Click on the Start button, point to **Settings** and then click on **Taskbar**.
- Click on the **Start Menu Programs** index tab.
- Click on the button marked **Remove**.
- Scroll to the bottom of the **Remove Shortcuts/Folders** list.
- Click on the shortcut icon you want to remove.
- Click on the **Remove** button at the bottom of the box.
- Click on the **Close** button.
- Close the **Taskbar Properties** dialog box.

To delete a shortcut from the Desktop:

- Click on the shortcut icon to select it.
- Press the **DELETE** key.
- Answer **Yes** when asked if you want to send the icon to the Recycle Bin.

  If the shortcut icon represents a file that is on a floppy disk, that file cannot be sent to the Recycle Bin. The file will be deleted.

Activity 8.3: Removing Shortcuts

1. To remove the Notepad shortcut, click on the Start button and point to **Settings**.

2. Click on **Taskbar**.

3. Click on the index tab for **Start Menu Programs**.

4. Click on **Remove**.

5. Scroll the list of programs to reach the bottom.

6. Click on the listing for the **Notepad** shortcut (see Figure 8-7).

   Do not continue with Step 7 unless you are certain it is the Notepad shortcut you have selected. You do not want to remove any other listing from the Start Menu!

7. Click on the **Remove** button.

8. Click on the **Close** button.

9. Click on **OK** to close the **Taskbar Properties** dialog box.

10. To remove the WordPad shortcut from the Desktop, click on the shortcut to select it.

11. Press the **DELETE** key.

12. Answer **Yes** to send the file to the Recycle Bin.

13. Close any other windows that are open.

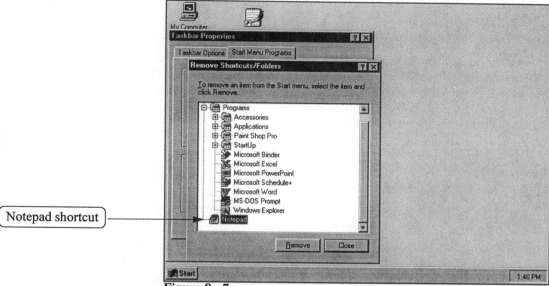

Figure 8 - 7

14. Leave *Windows 95* open for the next activity.

LOCATING A FILE IN WINDOWS 95

The instructions in Activities 8.1 and 8.2 told you where to find the Notepad and WordPad icons so that you could create shortcuts. But what if you had no help? How can you create a shortcut icon if you cannot find the original icon for that file?

The answer lies in the **Find** feature, which is reached from the Start menu. The **Find** feature lets you type in as much as you know about the file you are looking for, and then displays all the matching listings.

To locate a file using Find:

- Click on the Start button and click on **Find**.

- Click on **Files or Folders**.

- In the box marked **Named:**, type as much of the filename as you know. If you do not know the entire file name, type the letters you know followed by an asterisk (*).

- In the box marked **Look In:**, if you know the drive or folder that contains the file you are looking for, choose it from the list. If you know the drive but not the folder, choose the drive from the list and check the box marked **Include subfolders**. If you do not know the drive *or* folder, choose **My Computer** from the list and make sure the **Include subfolders** box is checked.

- Click on the button marked **Find Now**.

- Click on the **View** menu and make sure that **Details** has been chosen. If not, click on **Details** so that you can see complete information about the files.

- Examine the list of files that appears at the bottom of the box. Look at the **Type** of each. The file you are seeking should be on the list. Its location will be listed in the column marked **In Folder**. If more than one file has the same name, look at the details about the file. To create a shortcut icon for a program, you will be looking for a file listed as an *application*.

Activity 8.4: Finding a file

In this activity you will locate the file that runs WordPad. You will assume that the file is somewhere on your hard disk, but you do not know which folder contains it. If the file is on your network drive, not your hard disk, ask your instructor or lab assistant for help.

1. Click on the Start menu and point to Find.

2. Click on **Files or Folders**.

3. Click on the **Name & Location** index tab.

4. In the **Named:** text box type: **WordPad**

5. The box marked **Look In:** should contain the listing for the hard drive (**C:**). If not, change the listing.

6. The box marked **Include subfolders** should be checked (Figure 8-8). If not, check it.

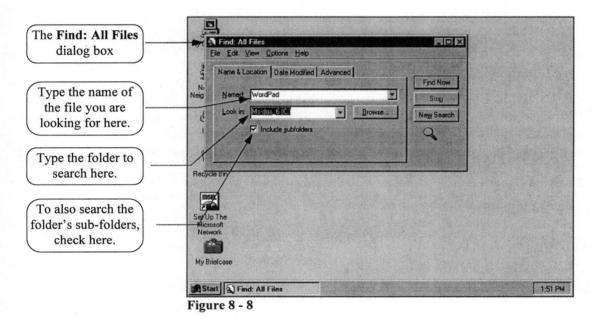

The **Find: All Files** dialog box

Type the name of the file you are looking for here.

Type the folder to search here.

To also search the folder's sub-folders, check here.

Figure 8 - 8

7. Click on the **Find Now** command button.

    All files that match what you typed will be listed at the bottom of the box (see Figure 8-9).

    *The file you are looking for is an **application** file (a file that runs a program). The last file on the list matches this description.*

 PROBLEM SOLVER: *If you do not see the size and type of file listed, click on the **View** menu and click on **Details**.*

 PROBLEM SOLVER: *If the file is not listed, it may be located on the network drive, not the hard drive. Open the **Look in:** box, and select the network drive. If you need help with this step, ask your instructor or lab assistant.*

8. Click on the *WordPad* file that lists its type as *application*.

9. To create a shortcut, drag the icon to the Desktop and release the mouse button.

10. Close the **Find** dialog box.

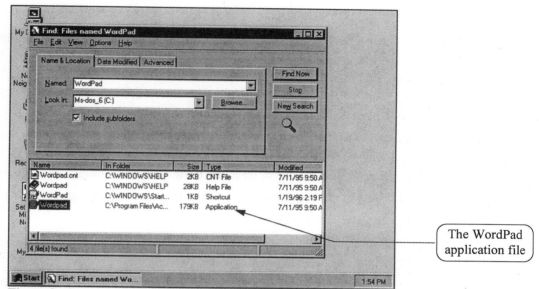

Figure 8 - 9   **Results of the Search**

11. To test the shortcut, double-click on the shortcut to start *WordPad*.

12. Close *WordPad*.

13. Delete the WordPad shortcut from the desktop and send it to the Recycle Bin.

14. Leave your computer running for the next activity.

SUMMARY

In Lesson 8 you learned what a shortcut is. You learned to create shortcuts to place those shortcuts on the Start menu and on the Desktop. You learned how to locate the files that run various programs by using the **Find** feature. Finally, you learned to remove the shortcuts you created.

KEY TERMS

Application	Folders	Sub-folders
Details	Shortcut	
Find	Shortcut icon	

INDEPENDENT PROJECTS

These projects will give you practice in creating and removing shortcuts, as well as using the **Find** feature.

Independent Project 8.1: Creating a Shortcut for a program

In this project you will create a shortcut for Solitaire. You will place the shortcut on the Start menu.

1. Run *Windows 95* if it is not already open.

2. Double-click on the **My Computer** icon on the desktop.

3. Double-click on the listing for the hard disk (drive **C:**) of your computer.

4. Scroll the **C:** window and double-click on the folder called **Windows**.

5. Scroll the **Windows** window and click on the file called **Sol** which is preceded by an icon of a deck of cards in a box. You may remember this icon from the Solitaire window.

6. Drag the icon down to the Taskbar and position it on top of the Start button.

7. Click on the Start button to make sure the shortcut is there.

8. With the Start menu open, press **PRINTSCREEN** to copy an image of the Start menu to the Clipboard.

9. Run WordPad and click on **EDIT/Paste** to place the image into a document.

10. Unselect the image and press **CTRL+END** to reach the end of the document.

11. Type your name and the date.

12. Print the document and close WordPad without saving.

13. Close all open windows.

14. To test the shortcut, open the Start menu and click on the **Solitaire** shortcut to run the game.

15. Close Solitaire.

16. To remove the shortcut, click on the **Start** button, point to **Settings** and click on **Taskbar**.

17. Click on the **Start Menu Programs** index tab.

18. Click on Remove.

19. Scroll down the list of programs. Solitaire should be the last item.

20. Click on Solitaire and then click on Remove.

21. Click on the **Close** button.

22. Close the Taskbar Properties box.

23. Click on the Start button to make sure that the shortcut has been removed.

24. Close any open windows so that the Desktop is clear.

Independent Project 8.2: Using the Find feature

In this project, you will practice using the **Find** feature to locate the file that runs the **Paint** program. When you have located it, you will create and then remove a shortcut for the program.

1. Use the **Find** feature to locate the program file for the **Paint** program.

   Remember that you are looking for an application file (see Figure 8-10). If you need help, refer back to Activity 8.4, Steps 1-7.

2. As soon as you locate the file, place a shortcut for Paint on the Desktop.

   For help, refer back to Activity 8.4, Steps 8-9.

3. Next, use **Find** to locate that runs the Explorer. Place a shortcut for the Windows Explorer on the Desktop. HINT: See Activity 8.4.

4. Double-click on each of the new shortcuts to run the programs.

   If either of the shortcuts is covered by an open window on the Desktop, drag the window out of the way.

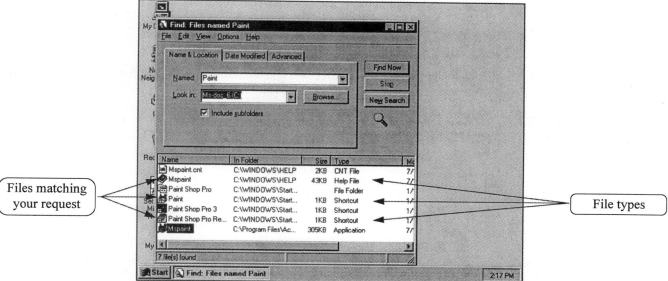

Figure 8 - 10

5. Close all open windows.

6. Close the Paint and Explorer windows.

7. Use **PRINTSCREEN** to print a picture of the Desktop with the Paint and Explorer shortcuts. Include your name and the date on the document.

8. Close WordPad without saving the document.

9. Remove each shortcut from the Desktop by sending it to the Recycle Bin.

Independent Project 8.3: Creating Shortcuts for a Floppy Drive and a Hard Drive

In this project, you will put shortcuts for the floppy drive containing your data disk and the hard drive on the Desktop. You will test the shortcuts, and then you will send them to the Recycle Bin.

1. Turn on your computer, if it is not already on.

2. Double-click on the **My Computer** icon.

3. In the **My Computer** window, click on the icon for the floppy drive that contains your data disk.

4. Create a shortcut for the icon by dragging it to the Desktop with the *right mouse button.*

5. Click on **Create Shortcut Here**.

6. Create a shortcut for the hard drive in the same way.

7. Close the **My Computer** window.

8. Press **PRINTSCREEN** to send an image of your Desktop containing the two new shortcuts to the Clipboard.

9. Run WordPad and click on **EDIT/Paste** to bring the image into WordPad.

10. Unselect the image in WordPad, press **CTRL+END**, and type your name at the bottom of the screen.

11. Print a copy of the document.

12. Close WordPad without saving the document.

13. Test each shortcut by double-clicking on it and then close the window that opens. Make sure your data disk is in the floppy drive.

14. Remove both shortcuts from the Desktop by sending them to the Recycle Bin.

15. Exit properly from *Windows 95*.

Appendix 1

FORMATTING A DISK

Formatting a disk means preparing it so that it can be used to save documents. Most people today purchase pre-formatted disks. This makes the formatting task unecessary. However, sooner or later, everyone who uses a personal computer will come across an unformatted disk, or will need to reformat an old disk. Therefore, learning how to format a disk makes good sense.

In *Windows 95* disk formatting is done at the **My Computer** window.

To format a disk:

- From the Desktop, double-click on the **My Computer** icon

    *The **My Computer** window appears on the screen (Figure A-1). There is an icon for each of the drives on your computer, plus icons for the Control Panel and Printers.*

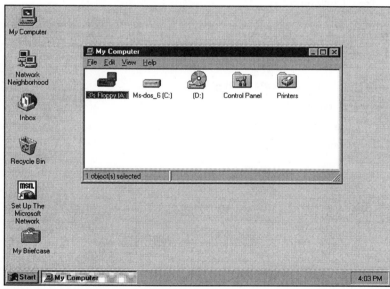

Figure A - 1

- Place an unformatted disk in the floppy drive.

    You may format an unformatted disk or you may reformat an old disk. Formatting a diskette erases all information on the disk. Make sure you insert an unformatted diskette or a diskette that has information you don't want into the drive.

- Click once on the icon for the drive in which the disk is located.

    ✓ **PROBLEM SOLVER:** *Make sure you **DO NOT** double-click on the drive icon. If you do, Windows 95 will attempt to read the drive.*

- Click on **FILE/Format**.

    *The **Format** dialog box appears on the screen (Figure A-2).*

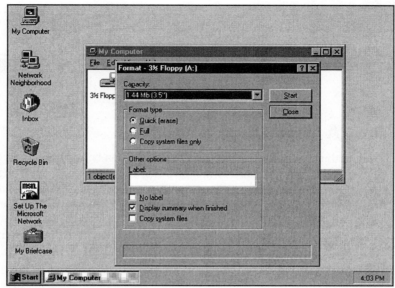

Figure A - 2

- Select the desired capacity, format type, and other options.

- Click on **Start**.

    The formatting process begins. When the formatting process is over, a dialog box will appear with the Format Results.

- Click on **Close**.

- Close the **Format** dialog box.

- Close the **My Computer** window.

    NOTE: *You will not format a diskette now. The purpose of this section is for future reference.*

Appendix 2

USING SHORTCUT KEYS WITH WINDOWS 95

Use the following keys to perform actions in *Windows 95*. Other key combinations have been presented in Lessons 1 and 5.

Action	Shortcut Keys
Selecting a menu	ALT + underlined letter
Selecting a menu item	ALT + underlined letter
Creating a new file	CTRL + N
Opening a file	CTRL + O
Saving a file	CTRL + S
Printing a file	CTRL + P
Undoing an action	CTRL + Z
Cutting an item	CTRL + X
Copying an item	CTRL + C
Pasting an item	CTRL + V
Selecting all of a document	CTRL + A
Moving from item to item in a dialog box	TAB
Moving within a list in a dialog box	↑ or ↓
Selecting OK in a dialog box	ENTER
Selecting Cancel in a dialog box	ESC
Switching among programs on the Desktop	ALT + TAB

USING THE KEYBOARD TO OPERATE THE MOUSE

Windows 95 provides an option called **MouseKeys** for moving the mouse pointer with the keyboard. This option is useful if there is no mouse attached to your computer or you do not like using the mouse. Turn **MouseKeys** on at the Accessibility Options window, which is reached from the Control Panel. Once **MouseKeys** is turned on, use the numeric keypad to operate the mouse.

To turn on MouseKeys:

- Make sure the numeric keypad is turned on.
- Double-click on the Accessibility Options icon in the Control Panel window.
- Click on the **Mouse** index tab.
- Click in the **Use MouseKeys** check box so that a check appears.
- Click **OK**.

  A mouse icon will appear next to the date on the Taskbar. Now you will be able to use the numeric keypad as well as the mouse itself to operate the mouse pointer.

To Move and Click the Mouse using MouseKeys:

- To move the mouse pointer, press the arrow keys on the numeric keypad.

- To click the mouse, press the **5** on the numeric keypad.

- To double-click the mouse, press the + on the numeric keypad.

Index